D0282439

Sexually Speaking

What Every Woman Needs to Know about Sexual Health

Dr. Ruth K. Westheimer

Amos Grunebaum, M.D., and Pierre Lehu

WILEY

John Wiley & Sons, Inc.

The information contained in this book is not intended to serve as a replacement for professional medical advice. Any use of the information in this book is at the reader's discretion. The author and the publisher specifically disclaim any and all liability arising directly or indirectly from the use or application of any information contained in this book. A health care professional should be consulted regarding your specific situation.

For general information about our other products and services, please contact our Customer Care Department within the United States at (800) 762-2974, outside the United States at (317) 572-3993 or fax (317) 572-4002.

Wiley also publishes its books in a variety of electronic formats and by print-on-demand. Some content that appears in standard print versions of this book may not be available in other formats. For more information about Wiley products, visit us at www .wiley.com.

ISBN 978-0-470-64335-8; ISBN 978-1-118-11934-1 (ebk.);
ISBN 978-1-118-11935-8 (ebk.); ISBN 978-1-118-11936-5 (ebk.)

Printed in the United States of America
10 9 8 7 6 5 4 3 2 1

One who is afraid to ask questions will never learn.
—*Rabbi Moses Maimonides (1125–1204),*
Laws of Torah Studies

You will have a great job forever, as long as people have sex. Everyone is doing it, no matter their skin color or whether they are rich or poor. And they will never stop having sex.
—*Freddi Grunebaum, circa 1977, when he first heard his son Amos Grunebaum was planning to become an obstetrician*

CONTENTS

PREFACE

When clients come to my office for sex therapy, very often I must send them to see a medical doctor first to rule out any physical causes for their problems. If the client is a woman, I send her to see her gynecologist. I've always looked at women's sexuality as a team effort between my work and that of the medical community. In this book, I get the chance to demonstrate what such a team can do.

Luckily for me, my coauthor is a doctor who considers it an important part of his care to ensure that his patients' sex lives are fully functional. Dr. Amos Grunebaum and I are old friends, and we get along so well not just because we both hail from Germany but because of our understanding that optimal sexual functioning is an important component of a woman's overall health. Sadly, not every gynecologist makes the same effort that Dr. Amos does with regard to sexual functioning. Because of this, women need to have a better understanding of what to expect when going to a gynecologist, for both their physical and their sexual well-being, so that they can get the help they require.

I've always regretted that because of the Nazis, I never got to fulfill my dream of becoming a medical doctor. Yet although I admire doctors, I've had my share of those who've given me the wrong advice. Doctors aren't perfect, and the various pressures they now face can make it even more difficult for them. This is why every woman needs to take more responsibility for her own health. I have visited a gynecologist many times, and I didn't always have

viii   Preface

the information I needed to ensure that I was getting the very best care. In preparing this book, I've learned a lot about what these visits can offer, so I know my readers will as well. Whether you currently have a problem with your sex life or are simply interested in getting the most from your visits to the gynecologist, I hope that you and every other woman will want to have this book as a resource.

—Dr. Ruth K. Westheimer

My practice is based in one of the best hospitals in the world, New York Hospital–Cornell University Medical Center in Manhattan. We offer women the most up-to-date and effective technologies for their gynecological care. If I need to refer a woman to a specialist, one of the best doctors is probably working just down the hall. Of course, I realize that not every gynecologist has access to this type of facility, and it's the patients of those doctors who need this book the most. If you're sure that your medical issue is fairly routine, then you can usually trust that you are getting adequate care. Yet if you don't know how to ask questions and what questions to ask, you might fall into a situation where you require the best possible care but aren't getting it. It's not necessarily the doctor's fault. It's difficult to suggest to patients that they travel hundreds of miles to get medical care when quite possibly it wouldn't make a difference. A doctor needs to have confidence in his or her skills and in the available facilities. It's up to patients to seek out the information they need so that they can make informed decisions.

There is, however, one area of a woman's health that could use improvement in hospitals big and small. The Victorian attitude, the idea that sex is something to be buried under the rug, is much stronger in this country than in my native Germany. For me, it is natural to talk to my patients about their sexual functioning, though I must admit that some are embarrassed when I first open up this line of questioning. Yet because I am in charge of helping women with their pregnancies, which, of course, could not happen without sex, I see no reason not to treat sex as an important component of a woman's total health.

Dr. Ruth and I collaborated on another book, *Dr. Ruth's Pregnancy Guide for Couples*, and that was quite a satisfying experience for me. Here we get to broaden our scope, covering every aspect of what a gynecologist has to offer his or her patients, and I hope that together we will change the attitude of women all across the country with regard to how they view their relationship with their gynecologists.

—Amos Grunebaum, M.D.

ACKNOWLEDGMENTS

To the memory of my entire family who perished during the Holocaust. To the memory of my late husband, Fred, who encouraged me in all of my endeavors. To my daughter, Miriam Westheimer, Ed.D.; son-in-law, Joel Einleger, M.B.A.; their children, Ari and Leora; my son, Joel Westheimer, Ph.D.; daughter-in-law, Barbara Leckie, Ph.D.; and their children, Michal and Benjamin. I have the best grandchildren in the entire world!

Special thanks to my friend and coauthor Amos Grunebaum, M.D., and to Pierre Lehu, my minister of communications, with whom I have now collaborated on more than fifteen books.

Thanks to all of the many family members and friends who add so much to my life. I'd need an entire chapter to list them all, but some must be mentioned here: Michael Banks, M.D.; David Best, M.D.; Frank Chervenak, M.D.; Chuck Blazer; Richard Cohen, M.D.; Mike Glazer, Ph.D.; David Hryck, Esq.; Rabbi and Mrs. Barry Katz; Bonnie Kaye; Robert Krasner, M.D.; Marga and Bill Kunreuther; Steve Lassonde; Matthew and Vivian Lazar; Rabbi and Mrs. William Lebeau; Peter Niculescu; Rabbi and Mrs. James Ponet; Lesile Rahl; Amir Shaviv; Jerome Cliff Rubin; Daniel Schwartz; Joanne Seminara, Esq.; David Simon, M.D.; Jerome Singerman, Ph.D.; Dr. and Mrs. William Sledge; and Jeffrey Tabak, Esq.

And to everyone at John Wiley & Sons who made this book possible, starting with Stephen Kippur, Tom Miller, Christel Winkler, and Jorge Amaral.

—Dr. Ruth K. Westheimer

To the memory of my parents, Rachel and Freddi. As Holocaust survivors they instilled in me a desire to do better and find a profession that I loved. It was my father who told me when he heard about my decision to become an obstetrician that I would have a job forever, "as long as people have sex." Nothing could be more true.

To my daughter, Emma, sister, Gabi, brother-in-law, Sasha, and niece, Oona.

Special thanks to my friend and coauthor Dr. Ruth Westheimer and to Pierre Lehu.

Thank you also to all of those who have added so much to my life, especially to all of my patients, nurses, and coworkers who have taught me so much over the last decades. Without them, I would be much less.

Thanks to New York-Presbyterian Hospital and Weill Cornell Medical College for their support, and especially to Frank Chervenak, M.D., who has been supporting me and pushing me forward for the last ten years. Not a day passes by when he does not remind me (in person, on the phone, or by e-mail): "Write more, publish more, Amos; you can do it!"

And to everyone at John Wiley & Sons, including Stephen Kippur, Tom Miller, Christel Winkler, and Jorge Amaral.

—Amos Grunebaum, M.D.

Introduction

Once upon a time a woman went to see her doctor. She was greeted by a smiling man who took his time when examining her. When she left, she was absolutely sure that he had everything under control, and she didn't have to worry about a thing. This isn't the opening line of a fairy tale but the way the doctor/patient experience used to be not so long ago. This isn't to say that serious medical issues were always treatable, but one's health was put into the confident hands of a doctor, and that was that. The idea of questioning a doctor would never have occurred to a patient. Doctors were looked on as if they were gods who knew all there was to know.

Not only have there been tremendous medical advances since those days, but many other changes have taken place, such as women having the choice of seeing a male or a female gynecologist. Most of these changes have improved the doctor-patient relationship, but, as we all know, with progress comes responsibility. Now individuals need to be responsible for knowing a lot more in order to get the most out of our modern health-care system. Helping women get optimal care when they see a gynecologist is the aim of this book.

One major change that took place is the near disappearance of the GP, the general practitioner. Yes, GPs still exist, but these days unless you are dealing with the common cold, you're likely to be sent to a specialist at the drop of a hat. On one hand, that can be a good thing, because a specialist really knows his or her stuff. On the other hand, when you're seeing a myriad number of doctors, you can get lost in the shuffle. For women, however, that doesn't have to be the case. Your gynecologist is equipped to deal with many of the medical issues you might encounter, and if you hunt around, you can find a gynecologist who will supervise your overall health. An important goal of this book is to help you stop categorizing a gynecologist as only a doctor who deals with "down there" but rather as a woman's doctor who can guide you in a variety of ways.

One area that women need medical help with is their sexual functioning, and their gynecologist should be their first line of support. Yet because sex is an embarrassing subject, this area often gets neglected. Even worse, some women never go to see a gynecologist, or they wait until it can't be put off any longer, because they feel too embarrassed or uncomfortable exposing their bodies. Routine care is important to prevent and treat problems before they develop into more serious issues. Together, we hope to explain not only what a gynecologist can do for you but also how you can get over your fears and integrate yourself into the process in order to get the most from your visits.

Just remember that our advice has to be general in nature. When a doctor sees a patient, dozens and maybe hundreds of factors must be weighed. A major lesson of this book isn't which treatment you should get for a particular medical issue but rather how to get the best possible treatment from your medical practitioners.

We want to give you the confidence to demand the best possible care, so you have to be armed with enough knowledge about what constitutes good medical care. That's what you'll get in this book.

The other important lesson we want to pass on is that your gynecologist can offer you much broader care than simply for your female anatomy. Gynecologists receive well-rounded medical training and can handle many of your health-related needs. This is another reason that it is important to develop a good relationship with your gynecologist. You should be able to rely on him or her to maintain your overall health. Certainly, there are situations where a specialist has to be called in, but once you establish a solid rapport with your gynecologist, you'll have a valuable ally.

If you have a significant other in your life, then you know that while sex isn't the only basis for your relationship, sex can strengthen that bond. Similarly, by opening up to your gynecologist regarding the sexual aspects of your health, you'll form a bond that can serve you well. Yes, you may be embarrassed to reveal that you have problems in your sex life, but once you do, you'll be on the road to having not only the best sex possible but also the best medical care overall.

1

How to Have a Happy, Healthy Sex Life

Probably more people are having some sort of sexual difficulty on any given day than have the common cold, yet good information about a problem related to sex is so much more difficult to obtain. In this chapter I'll give you some basic tips on how to have a happy, healthy sex life.

I've been writing about sex for some thirty years now, and so many people have told me how I've helped them improve their sex lives. Here's hoping I can do the same for you. Sadly, too many doctors in the United States are not given the proper training in talking about sexual matters with their patients. They don't learn it in medical school or during their training as gynecologists. We seem stuck with too many prurient attitudes left over from the Victorian era, so instead of simply considering sex a part of our daily lives that deserves the same attention as any other bodily function, we act as if sex is shameful and something not to be discussed, even with a doctor whose field includes all of the organs involved in proper sexual functioning.

As you know, I talk about sex from morning till night and have been doing it publicly for more than a quarter of a century, yet even I still get embarrassed sometimes. From time to time, I have to force myself to say the words *vagina* or *orgasm* or *masturbation*. In fact, when I give a lecture, I usually get the audience to say those words out loud because it helps break the ice. So I fully appreciate the reticence that a doctor might have about the subject of sex, and I certainly understand any embarrassment you might feel. Yet while most people get sickened at the sight of blood, doctors learn to get over such feelings, and surgeons can cut open a body without thinking twice about it. I don't blame doctors for their lack of training on sex, but I do blame the medical establishment, which doesn't offer the proper training to young doctors. Although I've been calling for doctors to have more training for many years now, even when I do grand rounds at hospitals and speak to the doctors, young residents still tell me that the training they get in the area of sex remains lackluster, to put it gently.

You could potentially excuse this state of affairs by saying that a lack of sexual knowledge isn't life threatening, and as long as a couple can reproduce, it's just not that important and so not an area that doctors need to cover very thoroughly. But you'd be wrong, because, of course, sex is important. It's part of the glue that holds a relationship together. A sexless marriage is not a stable one. If you're in an unhappy marriage, you'll be under a lot of stress, and stress has definite negative consequences on your health.

Sexual problems can also make it more difficult to actually form relationships. Both men and women who have sexual problems may find themselves alone, and although being single is not life threatening, either, it certainly affects the quality of your life as much or more than many other illnesses. How many people would give up having a life partner in exchange for getting rid of their hay fever, for example? If people think sex is important, then so should the medical community.

Then there's the question of sexually transmitted diseases (STDs), which can not only do great damage to your body but can also be life threatening. If doctors are not involved in their patients' sex lives, then whatever message they try to pass on regarding STDs will not get through. If patients are afraid to talk about sexual matters with their doctors, they may not bring up STDs, either. STDs, without a shadow of a doubt, affect a gynecologist's practice. To give but one example, it is vital to know whether a pregnant patient has herpes.

Although I shouldn't need to prove that good sexual functioning is important and should be assisted by the medical community, there is no escaping the fact that as a whole, women do not get the support they need because the topic of sex continues to be one that doctors are not properly trained to handle. While in some instances it helps if the gynecologist is a woman, just the fact that a female doctor is speaking to a female patient does not ensure that good communication about sex is taking place. In fact, some women may feel more comfortable talking to a male doctor about certain issues, including sex.

Patients could help change this situation. If doctors were faced with daily questions about sexual functioning, they would get used to answering them, and they would study the sexual issues they were being asked about. Yet patients also feel embarrassed, so they don't raise the questions they have about sexual functioning. This combined embarrassment of both doctors and patients makes the topic so rarely part of the doctor/patient relationship.

Hopefully, by reading this book, you'll have a better idea of what to do to get the help you need from your doctor. If you are a doctor reading this book, maybe you will learn to change the way you handle your patients' sexual problems. The door of communication between patient and doctor can't be opened until patients have a good understanding of their own sexual functioning, so that's what I'm going to tackle first.

Orgasm

Because it is required for a man to have an orgasm in order for our species to reproduce, evolution has made certain that most men don't have a problem in that department. But a woman can get pregnant without ever having an orgasm, so it is far more common to find women who encounter difficulties when trying to achieve sexual satisfaction. Yet the very fact that women can have orgasms even though these are not needed for reproduction tells you that orgasms are important to a woman's well-being. The clitoris is the seat of a woman's potential to have an orgasm, and the fact that every woman is born with a clitoris means that every woman should be able to have an orgasm.

While on rare occasions there are women who cannot have orgasms because of some physical reason (most often a disease, such as diabetes, or severe depression), for the most part the two main causes of a woman's inability to have an orgasm are either ignorance or psychological problems or a combination of the two. Both of these factors are well within the purview of a gynecologist's expertise.

We've all seen couples making love in the movies. The man is on top of the woman, and the two are thrusting at each other, both having tremendous orgasms. If a couple bases their own lovemaking on what they've seen on screen, they would assume that both partners would always have an orgasm from intercourse in the missionary position, that is, with the man on top. Now some couples can do this, but the majority of women do not get enough clitoral stimu-lation from this type of intercourse to have an orgasm. As a result of this mistaken belief, in millions of bedrooms couples are having sex and the woman is not having an orgasm. Because so many women blame themselves for this situation, thinking that they are deficient in some way, they end up faking orgasms, which guarantees that this nonorgasmic sex life will continue forever or at least as long as the woman is with this particular partner.

The cure for this situation is simple. Some women will become sufficiently aroused from foreplay, by which I mean manual or oral stimulation to her clitoris, along with other caresses and kisses before intercourse, to actually have an orgasm during intercourse. Other women need continuous direct physical stimulation to their clitoris in order to have an orgasm, and this can be done either before, during (when using positions other than the missionary), or after intercourse by her partner using his fingers, his mouth, his big toe, or a vibrator.

Some women cannot figure out what exact sensations they need to have orgasms with a partner. In fact, they may need to concentrate so much in order to become sufficiently aroused that they can only have an orgasm alone via masturbation, and for some, masturbation must include the very strong sensations of a vibrator. Many of these women can then teach their partners what to do, although a small percentage end up being able to have an orgasm only by themselves, because the distraction of having someone else with them is too disruptive to their concentration.

Having read the previous information, you may think you now know everything you need to about having orgasms, and you may wonder why you should talk to your doctor about your sex life. We'll get to some of the physical reasons that you might need a doctor's help, but let's address this particular issue here. How many people who know they have to lose weight don't go on a diet-and-exercise plan until after their doctor orders them to? How many people begin flossing their teeth only because they're following the instructions of their dentist? One could bring up dozens of other examples, such as reducing salt intake, using condoms, stopping tobacco use, and so on. A doctor is an authority figure, and some people need that extra boost of hearing their doctor tell them to do something for their own good before they can motivate themselves to do it. After all, every woman who fakes orgasms whenever she has sex knows that she isn't having orgasms. These women should just tell their partners and figure out what to do, but instead they prefer to go on faking orgasms. Yet certainly some of these women, if their gynecologists asked about their sex lives, listened to their stories, went over some of this information, and handed them a pamphlet, would then take action to start having orgasms. That would be especially true if their doctors asked them about it again at the next visit.

When you talk to your doctor about an issue, it changes your perspective on it. You may live with a nagging pain for years, but once you report it to your doctor, you'll take whatever action is needed to get rid of that pain—you'll go for X-rays, you'll undergo physical therapy, or you'll take a pain reliever. If your doctor tells you to do something, you're more likely to listen. So it is with sexual matters. If you could discuss whatever is wrong with your sex life with your gynecologist, the odds increase significantly that you will take action to improve it. But if your doctor doesn't bring it up, and if you don't raise the issue, then that will never happen and the problem could go on forever.

From Dr. Amos's Office: Talking about Sex

Patients rarely, if ever, volunteer to tell their obstetrician/gynecologist (Ob/Gyn) about their sex lives. That's why I make a point of asking my patients about this. Some find it a great relief and open right up, and usually I can help them. Others are shocked and just mumble something like, "It's fine." I can often tell by their responses that it's not fine, but they're simply not willing to discuss it with me. That's okay, but I've also noticed that if I bring it up again, they will sometimes be more likely to open up a bit. Because they don't expect me to ask them about their sex lives, it comes as a bit of a shock the first time, and rather than give me an honest answer, they duck the question. Yet once they know ahead of time that I'm going to ask them this question, then some of these women prepare themselves. Before they get to my office, they go back and forth in their minds as to whether they should say something, and many times they end up giving me at least a partial picture of what's going on. Once the door is open, I can usually offer them some solutions to whatever the problem might be or refer them to someone else who can. Getting the right information about sex is especially important for pregnant women because of all of the misinformation and myths about sex during pregnancy. More about this later.

My situation is the opposite of what Dr. Amos faces because people who come to see me expect to talk about their sex lives. Yet that doesn't mean they won't lie. Plenty of women won't reveal that they've been faking orgasms the first time we talk or at least at the beginning of the session. But I can usually tell what's actually taking place in their bedrooms because their stories don't make sense. I guess that they must be faking orgasms, and then when I confront them, most of the time they let down their defenses. So, you see, even when people come to see me because they admit that they have sex problems, they still find it difficult to talk about the details of their sex lives.

I'm not trying to provide you with excuses or let you off the hook with these examples. I just want you to understand that it will probably take some effort on your part to talk openly about your sex life with your doctor. Another thing is that the older you are, the harder it is to talk about your sex life. Younger women have become much more open and will discuss their sexual functioning with greater ease with their doctors or with almost anyone. That's great because by sharing information, everyone gets to have better sex. This can also put pressure on some people, though; just because more people are talking about having sex doesn't mean that everyone has a partner with whom to have sex. If all of your girlfriends are going over the nitty-gritty of their sex lives in front of you and you don't have a partner, that will make you feel deficient. But finding a partner is the subject of another book because doctors have enough to do without also becoming matchmakers!

Peer pressure can play an even greater role with teenagers. If you're the mother of a teenage girl, you have to be aware that all of the talk about sex will push her into wanting to have sex to keep up with everyone else. A visit to the gynecologist will inject a heavy dose of reality into the picture, and a doctor can be a good ally. Your gynecologist won't tell you what was said during your daughter's appointment, but information will definitely be communicated that will sometimes sink in more deeply than if it comes from you.

Tips on How to Talk to Your Doctor about Sex

While I've said over and over that you should talk to your gyne-cologist about sexual issues, I've also admitted that it's not that easy. Here are some tips to help you.

The first is to write your questions down. If you send them to your doctor ahead of time, either by e-mail, fax, or snail mail, then your doctor won't be blindsided by them and will be prepared to answer your questions fully. Yet even if you don't send the list or hand it to the doctor, simply by having such a list you'll be clearer on what you want to say, just in case you get tongue-tied.

If you decide that you want to talk to your doctor without first giving him or her a written list, then I suggest you begin the conversation by saying that you want to talk about a sexual problem. Some doctors are unsure about how open you actually want to be, so they downplay sexual subjects. By saying that you want to talk about a sexual matter, not only are you setting the agenda, but you're also giving your doctor a minute or so to adapt his or her own mind-set to the subject. In other words, you might not be the only one who has to take a deep breath before having a sex talk. And don't just sit there in silence when your doctor gives you some advice. Thank your doctor for being willing to talk about sexual matters. Not every doctor needs to be encouraged, but you can never go wrong in giving praise where it is due.

You may run into a situation where your doctor is so embar-rassed that he or she gives your question an abrupt answer and then proceeds to steer the conversation elsewhere. I'm sorry to say this, but that's a cue to start looking for another doctor. A gynecologist is supposed to talk about sexual matters, and if yours isn't able to, and you have serious sexual questions, then you owe it to yourself to find another gynecologist who can answer them honestly and completely.

Although you certainly want only a doctor to perform medical procedures on you, when it comes to merely answering questions about sex, you might not need to ask the doctor. There's a very good chance that one or more of the nurses can answer your questions quite capably. In fact, a large practice of gynecologists or a hospital department probably has nurses whose main job is to answer patients' questions, and much of this information can be communicated over the phone. It's certainly less embarrassing to ask a question on the phone, and if the nurse either can't answer your question or feels that you really need to see the doctor, she'll let you know.

Don't be afraid to ask the nurse about anything at all, whether about sex or any other problem. If a doctor allows his or her nurses to answer patients' questions, you can be sure they have the proper training and are giving you correct information. If your question is too complicated for the nurse to handle, she'll know to either ask the doctor on your behalf or make an appointment for you to come in.

Other Issues

If bringing up the subject of sex is difficult, talking about ending an unintended pregnancy can be even harder. Just as our society is divided on the subject of abortion, so are the opinions of doctors. Doctors fall into several categories: those who perform abortions and will discuss that as an option; those who don't do abortions themselves but don't hesitate to recommend some other doctor who does; and doctors who are against abortions, don't do them, and also refuse to refer you to a doctor who might perform the abortion. The decision to have an abortion is often very difficult, and discussing it with your doctor can be stressful. Hopefully, if you want to have an abortion, you will never encounter a doctor who refuses to refer you to a doctor who does perform them. I strongly feel that it is a gynecologist's ethical responsibility to listen to a patient and respect her decision. Even though the doctor may be against abortion, I feel it is his or her duty to the patient to refer her to another doctor if she wants an abortion.

Patients come in various flavors as well, and certain women absolutely know what they want, while others aren't sure and wouldn't mind being talked out of getting an abortion.

When it comes to having an abortion, my advice is to call your doctor's office ahead of time and ask the person who answers the phone whether the doctor performs abortions, and then take it from there. If the doctor does not perform abortions, you can ask for a referral to a doctor who does. If you feel uncomfortable doing that, call your local family planning center, such as Planned Parenthood (you can find your local center at www.plannedparenthood.org) and ask for an appointment.

Although the pills that combat erectile dysfunction (ED)—Viagra, Levitra, and Cialis—are not under the purview of a gynecologist, these pills have changed the landscape for sex among older adults, so it is important that I comment on the subject.

These pills are not aphrodisiacs. They do not give a man the desire to have sex but only allow him to have an erection if he wants one. Where this can cause problems for a woman is when her partner has the desire and takes a pill and then wants to have sex, and she doesn't. Some of these pills are longer lasting, so turning a man down doesn't mean that he has wasted a pill, but even in that scenario, it's important that a couple talk about how they will integrate the use of such pills into their love life. A man who was having problems in this area and starts taking a pill so that his ability to have intercourse is suddenly rejuvenated will want to have sex more often. For at least a short while, the man's penis will become like a new toy and not the same organ he's had all of his life. Yet there could be many reasons that the woman in his life isn't ready to cooperate, and one of these could even be his new attitude, because it will seem to her that rather than wanting to make love to her, he's only interested in proving his new manhood to himself. Also, if their sex life had been waning, and she was concerned that part of the problem was her inability to arouse him, then having her partner go to the doctor to get a prescription for an ED pill without consulting her may have negative effects on her own sexual arousal.

The physical changes that happen to a couple as they age, not even considering any relationship issues, take place rather slowly. The number of times they make love a week or a month will slowly dwindle. Although perhaps the man isn't content with this new pattern, if they haven't discussed it, springing a surprise on her won't be very arousing and probably will have the opposite effect.

The solution is potentially very easy. All a couple has to do is talk about the situation and make the decision together for him to start taking pills. Obviously, the woman shouldn't withhold her permission unreasonably. If she wants to end their sex life, that's not really acceptable, because there's no reason to do so from a physical point of view. If she has any doubts about that, she should make an appointment with her gynecologist to discuss the coming change in her sex life. Her gynecologist should be able to reassure her that she can most certainly have sex safely and comfortably, providing she takes the proper precautions, such as using artificial lubrication.

As to pills that will increase a woman's level of desire, it seems that some progress has been made in that direction, but the FDA hasn't certified any of these as being safe, so at the time of writing this book, no such pill is actually available.

Up until now, we haven't found the etiology—the reason—for homosexuality. Nor have we found it for heterosexuality. More research needs to be done to find out why some people prefer their own sex to the opposite sex or are bisexual. Of course, lesbians also need gynecological care because they are subject to the same medical conditions as heterosexual women.

Lesbians can, of course, transmit sexual diseases and do have to be careful about contracting HIV/AIDS. It's true that the reports of cases of woman-to-woman transmission of HIV are rare, but that's because there may be other factors. For example, if a lesbian is a user of intravenous drugs or has also had sex with men, from a statistical point of view, she won't be considered to have contracted the disease from woman-to-woman contact, though it's possible that may have been the case. And while no penis may be involved, there have been cases where sex toys have been pointed out as the culprit in disease transmission.

The important point is that a lesbian should be just as diligent in reporting any risk factors she may have to her doctor as a woman who has sex only with men. A saying people used back in the 1980s was: "Women don't get AIDS, they just die from it." Protecting yourself from this risk is up to you. (I'll go into more detail about AIDS later in the book.)

Many lesbians do not necessarily mention their sexual orientation when seeing their gynecologists, afraid that they will encounter a negative reaction. Lesbians can get sexually transmitted diseases, although they are less likely to do so than heterosexual women. They are also less likely to require the services of a gynecologist because of a pregnancy, and, unless they are bisexual, they have no need of birth control, so in general lesbians will have less contact with their gynecologists. If they also don't talk about their sexuality, then lesbians might find that they get less care simply because they're so much less connected to their gynecologists.

Nevertheless, lesbians are as likely as heterosexual women to get gynecological conditions such as ovarian and uterine diseases or to have hormonal issues, so it's still important for them to see a gynecologist regularly.

Obviously, if a lesbian wants to be a mother and to be artificially inseminated, then she will often need the services of a specialist in that area.

My suggestion to lesbians is to be aware of these factors and make certain that you don't allow your sexual orientation to cause you to have any lower standard of care than a heterosexual woman does.

The Top Ten Ways Your Gynecologist Can Help Your Sex Life

1. Give you the right form of contraception so that you don't have to worry about an unintended pregnancy when having sex.

2. Keep you safe from sexually transmitted diseases.

3. Assist you in overcoming any difficulties you might have in achieving sexual satisfaction.

4. Help you alleviate any pain during sex.

5. Answer your questions about sexual functioning, thus giving you added confidence when having sex.

6. Explain to you the best methods of becoming pregnant so that sex doesn't become a chore when you and your partner try to conceive.

7. Tell you when and how you can engage in sex while pregnant.

8. Work with you to reestablish your sex life after giving birth.

9. Help you adapt to any changes in your sexual functioning brought on by perimenopause.

10. See that you can continue to enjoy an active sex life during your postmenopausal years.

Since I've written entire books on the subject of sex, I know I didn't cover every possible aspect of sex in this one chapter. If I was able to convince you to talk to your gynecologist about sex, however, I can be sure that you'll get all of the answers you need.

2

Everything You Wanted to Know about Your Vagina but Were Too Afraid to Ask

Some women are comfortable with their entire bodies, including their vaginas, while others are not. If you are not on good terms with this important part of your anatomy, you'll miss out on all that it has to offer you, as well as put yourself at risk for developing medical problems. So sit back and enjoy this chapter, as you soak up all of the information you'll need about your vagina.

No one would think it an exaggeration to say that women, more than men, spend a lot of time looking at themselves in the mirror. Most women could describe every wrinkle or spot on their faces. Yet when it comes to their intimate anatomy, many women are much less knowledgeable than men, whether about their visible genitalia or their inner workings.

Why is it important to have a better understanding of your genitals than, for example, how your stomach or liver works? (And I'm not saying that you shouldn't have a basic understanding of those and every other part of your body.) Mostly because you interact with your genitals regularly, which includes when having sex. Since what you do affects them, you need to know how they work in order to better influence your actions.

You also have another incentive to learn as much as possible about your body. Amazing advances have occurred in medicine, and surgeons can now repair damage to your body that was once impossible to even imagine. All of those medical advances provide you with options. In many cases, the old methods haven't been supplanted, but you have a wider array of choices. In addition, doctors no longer have as much time to spend with their patients. The old days of simply putting yourself in the hands of the doctor are over. To some extent, you'll have to take responsibility for making the ultimate decisions about your health care. Many procedures require you to sign a consent form, so, whether you like it or not, you'll be put in a position of having to consider your own treatment or that of a loved one. This is especially true of people in the so-called sandwich generation, who are often responsible for the care of both their children and their elderly parents.

After hearing all of the available options to treat your problem, you can still say, "Doc, I trust you, you decide." Yet it won't be as easy as before. Your relatives and friends will offer you their opinions, which will plant seeds of doubt in your mind. The nearest computer with its window into the Internet will lure you to look up information. In many cases, even your doctor will expect more of you than a "you make the decision" response, because so many patients take the opposite tack and want to be very involved. If you abandon all responsibility, at the very least you'll be left with a guilty conscience, and if matters don't turn out right, you could regret giving up control.

You're not expected to possess the medical knowledge of a doctor. To reach a final decision, you'll have to rely on your physician, to a great degree. When your doctor explains your choices, however, you should at least have a general idea about what's being discussed. If your gynecologist is talking about your ovaries, for example, you'll be a lot more comfortable if you know as much as possible about these organs and all the surrounding ones. Perhaps you were given some basic instruction in high school biology, but how much do you remember today? For those of you who do understand the basics of your reproductive anatomy, then you can skim this chapter looking for pieces of information you may not possess. If you're a bit hazy on the details, though (or perhaps you have a daughter you'd like to show this book to), I suggest you at least look at the diagrams, and if what you see isn't familiar, then spend a few more minutes studying the contents of this chapter.

Taking a Tour: The Vaginal Self-Examination

One of our greatest fears is the fear of the unknown. If you are not intimate with your own body and have no idea what the doctor is seeing, then that will make you more fearful. Yet if you've looked carefully at your vagina and do so on a regular basis, believe me when I tell you that you'll feel a lot better letting a doctor examine your vagina. I'm not saying that you won't be at all nervous, just a lot less nervous. If you take a deep breath and calm yourself down, what could be easier than looking at a part of your own anatomy?

I recommend that all women take a careful look at their genitalia, including their labia and vaginas. Although I've been addressing women who have not spent much time looking at their vaginas, there are other women who make a point of examining their genitalia and vaginas with some regularity. These examinations are called vaginal self-examinations (VSE), and they're not very dissimilar from examining your breasts. The point is to spot any differences in the appearance of your vagina. In a VSE, a woman inspects her vulva or external genitals, as well as her vagina and cervix, to become more familiar with her body and its functions. A VSE can help a woman learn more about her own body and occasionally find abnormalities.

You'll need the following items for a vaginal self-examination: a vaginal speculum, a mirror to check yourself, a flashlight or a lamp, clean hands (or gloves), and a lubricant. One way to do a VSE is by getting into a sitting position on your bed, with your back resting up against the headboard or the wall and your legs spread apart. Some women prefer to use the bathroom, putting one foot on top of the toilet. This position may make it a bit more difficult to hold the mirror and the flashlight, although some bathrooms are very well lit, and a flashlight isn't needed.

Employ whatever position works best for you, and angle the mirror in front of your vagina so that you can look at it. Open the lips and look inside. Find your clitoris and examine it. Find the urethra, the hole from which urine comes, which is located just inside the vaginal lips, and look at that. In other words, take an extensive tour that should last five to ten minutes. During the VSE, you can examine the following parts of the genitalia: the vagina, the vulva, the labia, the clitoris, the opening of the urethra, and the anus.

If you perform a VSE and notice any type of change, mark it down. It probably doesn't mean that you have to rush off to the gynecologist, but you should report it at the time of your next visit. Of course, if your VSE reveals something more significant, such as a lesion or several of them, make an appointment with your doctor for an exam as soon as possible.

What You Can See

Whether you've actually taken the vaginal tour or simply want to know more, here's a road map of what you'll see.

The mons pubis is a pad of fat that covers the pubic bone. (Nice of Mother Nature to provide a bumper for when you're having sex!)

From Dr. Amos's Office: Using Modern Technology

Many of my patients have complained that they are not flexible enough to bend down and self-examine their genitalia with a mirror. Here is a tip for doing a VSE in a more innovative, interactive way (I call it the iVSE): Use a webcam, one that sits on top of your computer and can be easily moved around (webcams that are built into laptops do not work as well). Hold the webcam in your hand (or place it on a tripod), position yourself comfortably, turn the webcam on, hold it where you want to look, and face the computer screen. You could also involve your husband or partner to help you with this examination. You can then see everything comfortably on the computer screen without being in an uncomfortable position. A webcam even takes pictures. Just be sure to heed these safety precautions: do this only in the privacy of your home; do not do it at work, and make sure the camera is not transmitting any images onto the Internet. Before starting, you may want to unplug the Internet cable or turn off the wireless to make sure the webcam is safe to use. If you don't have a webcam, you can use a digital camera. The advantage of digital pictures is that in most cameras, you can magnify them to see details.

If you're especially sensitive about your genitals, then at least for the first time, I give you permission not to touch anything but merely to look. I wouldn't want any woman to avoid the primary purpose of this exercise because she didn't want to touch her genitalia and her vagina or thought that this was somehow linked to masturbation (which this exam is not). Your vagina is not dirty, and it does not need to be cleansed. But if it would help any of you to wash your genitalia and the outside of your vagina first or to wear surgical gloves, then go right ahead. Hopefully, a little bit down the line you'll feel more comfortable and can loosen up and explore further.

The mons is covered with pubic hair, which can also add some more padding, although these days many women shave this area.

Directly below the mons are the labia, two separate sets of skin folds, one inside the other, that serve to protect and seal the vaginal opening. The outer set is called the labia majora (Latin for "large lips," and if you'd been born a male instead of a female, the same set of tissue would have turned into the scrotum, the sac that holds the testicles). The inner set of lips are called the labia minora ("small lips"), and while the majora are there to protect the overall vagina, the minora are there as a seal to keep things such as water and germs from getting inside the vagina. Although I use the word *vagina* to refer to the parts we see, the vagina is actually the internal organ within the lips, while the outer portion that is easily visible is called the vulva (see the illustrations in the appendix).

Just the way that no two people look exactly alike, the vulvas of women vary widely in appearance, in terms of both size and color (even the genitalia of twins may not look exactly the same). In some women, the labia minora lie within the labia majora, while in others they hang below. The color of the lips can vary from pink to flesh colored to light brown to dark brown. Because of this broad diversity, there is no such thing as a "normal"-looking vagina.

I find it strange to write about this, but it seems that some women are so concerned about the appearance of their vaginal lips that they undergo plastic surgery to "improve" them, which most of the time means making them smaller and more dainty.

The focus on the appearance of the vulva is the result, no doubt, of the increase in oral sex, especially among young people. It's the reason that so many women now shave their pubic hair. With men spending so much more time close to women's vulvas, it's understandable that women might worry about what their partners are seeing; however, this attitude is all wrong. It focuses on the superficial, rather than on what is important, the relationship. I would go so far as to say it actually detracts from forming a relationship. You can only concentrate on so many things at one time, and if men and women spend too much energy worrying about the appearance of their genitals, then that will only cause them to become self-centered and distracted from the relationship.

Similar to the lips of your mouth, the labia minora are covered with epithelium, a type of skin that is especially sensitive, which is one reason that having sex feels so good. The labia minora come together at the top of the vulva and form what is called the clitoral hood, a flap of skin that covers the clitoris, a woman's most important sexual organ.

The clitoris is made from a similar type of tissue as a penis, and when you are excited, it grows slightly and gets hard, just the way a penis does. It is the main seat of your sexual pleasure, and for most women, an orgasm is not possible unless she gets sufficient stimulus to her clitoris. Also like the penis, the tip of the clitoris is called the glans. You can see only the tip of the entire clitoris, the glans, while most of the clitoris lies beneath the skin and is called the shaft. The glans is filled with nerve endings, as is the area around the clitoris, making it very sensitive. The size and the shape of the glans vary greatly. When you are excited, the clitoris and the surrounding area fill with blood and the glans doubles in size. The surrounding tissue also grows larger so that it may be less exposed than when not aroused.

I know we are in the chapter on anatomy, not sex, but I felt it important to point out here that how much stimulation a woman prefers on her clitoris is not fixed. Some women need direct stimulation to have an orgasm, while others find direct stimulation actually painful and prefer for the stimulation to be done around the clitoris, not directly on it. Some women can have an orgasm from the indirect stimulation of the penis on the vaginal lips during intercourse, and many cannot. Each woman has to discover for herself which sensations produce an orgasm for her, and because her partner cannot guess, she needs to let him know, either verbally or by demonstration.

Urethra

The urethra is the tube that carries urine from the bladder in order for it to be excreted. The entrance to the urethra in women is located just below the clitoris and before the entrance to the vagina.

Vagina

The word *vagina* is Latin in origin and means "sheath" or "scabbard."
The vagina is the internal portion of the female genitalia. It begins
at the base of the labia minora and extends to the cervix, which is
the entrance to the uterus. The area at the opening of the vagina
is called the vestibule, and in young women it is covered by a
membrane called the hymen. Hymens are not uniform in shape,
and most of them have some sort of opening so that menstrual
blood can flow out of them, even if the hymen has not been
perforated. (In young women where the hymen does not have any
perforation, menstrual blood can back up into the vagina, causing
a very serious condition.)

The vagina is composed of three different types of tissue. The
outer layer, the part that you can touch, feels similar to the inside
of the mouth and is called the mucosa. Beneath the mucosa is
a layer of muscle, although most of it is concentrated toward
the entrance. Underneath that is fibrous tissue that connects the
vagina to other organs.

The vagina itself has few nerve endings, and those that it does
have are concentrated toward the front. When not in an excited
state, the top and the bottom come together so that it is flat.
An unaroused vagina is about three to five inches in length (the
interior wall is slightly longer than the back wall), although when
a woman is aroused, it lengthens a bit because of the inflow of
blood, which pushes the cervix farther backward.

The combination of tissues, muscle, and fibrous material allows
the vagina to expand so that it can contain a penis of any size, as
well as allow a baby to pass through. Also, the interior of the vagina
is not smooth but, rather, has folds. This extra material facilitates
its expansion during intercourse and birth.

Cervix

The cervix is the lower part of the uterus, dipping into the vagina.
Part of the cervix is visible during a pelvic exam and part lies

within the uterus. The cervix doesn't actually enter the vagina until puberty, resting entirely within the uterus until then. The center of the cervix is a small opening, and each end of it is called the os. The external os connects to the vagina, while the internal os connects to the cavity, the inside of the uterus. The shape of the external os changes, depending on whether a woman has had one or more vaginal deliveries or not. The cervix undergoes a change after a woman has had a vaginal birth, becoming a bit bulkier and more gaping. The cervix looks like a small round hole if the woman never had a baby, and its opening is larger and more like a line if she did have a baby. Menstrual blood flows from the uterus into the vagina via the cervix on its way out, and sperm swim up through the cervix into the uterus and toward a potential egg.

After menstruation ends, the os is blocked by mucus that is acidic and serves to stop sperm and bacteria from entering the uterus. Shortly before and during ovulation, this mucus changes, becoming more watery and less acidic, thus allowing sperm to penetrate and fertilize the egg. This kind of cervical mucus has the consistency of egg whites (some women refer to it as EWCM, egg white cervical mucus) and indicates that a woman is about to ovulate.

If the penis comes into contact with the cervix during intercourse, the woman may feel pain. Usually, this does not happen, but if the man's penis is particularly big or if he thrusts particularly deep, then his penis could touch the woman's cervix. If this occurs and she is in pain, she must speak up. Changing positions is usually effective, because varying the angle of penetration can keep the cervix out of reach. If the man is thrusting very strongly, he should use less force.

Uterus

The uterus is a pear-shaped organ, situated between the bladder and the rectum. It consists of a top part, the uterine body, and a bottom part, the cervix, which connects the body to the vagina. To the right and left of the uterine body are the fallopian tubes, which connect the uterus to the ovaries (see the illustrations in the appendix).

The uterus has a thick inner lining called the endometrium. Every month the endometrium reacts to the hormone estrogen, which is released by the ovaries, and begins to thicken as it gets ready for a fertilized egg to implant itself, where it will then grow into a baby. If no egg implants itself, then about fourteen days after ovulation the endometrial lining and the blood that caused the buildup are released, causing a woman to have her period. If a fertilized egg does attach itself to the endometrium in a process called implantation, the uterus will grow during the nine-month gestation period to accommodate the baby, and after the birth it will shrink back to a smaller size.

Does the uterus play any role in sex? Absolutely. When you are aroused, the uterus engorges with blood, much as the penis does, and that engorgement causes it to shift its position somewhat. In addition, very often during orgasm, the uterus contracts, which is something that can be felt by many women and contributes to their enjoyment of orgasm. A woman who has had her uterus removed during a hysterectomy may feel the absence of these contractions.

Fallopian Tubes

There are two fallopian tubes, a right one and a left one. Each fallopian tube has a funnel-shaped mouth, called the fimbriae, that sits just outside of each ovary, waiting to receive an egg. After ovulation, when an egg is expelled from the ovary, the egg enters one of the fallopian tubes through the fimbriated end. It is there that fertilization, the joining of the egg with the sperm, takes place. If the egg becomes fertilized, it starts to rapidly divide, first into the zygote, then the morula, and next the blastocyst, which develops into the embryo. This process takes place while the fertilized egg is propelled down through the tubes toward the uterine cavity by contractions of the tubes. The travel time within the fallopian tube to the uterus takes about five to seven days. Also inside the tubes are lots of microscopic hairs called cilia. These wave back and forth to help move any sperm that have made it into the tubes up toward a descending egg for fertilization.

Ovaries

You have two ovaries, situated on either side of your uterus. Each ovary is about the size of a walnut. It has follicles, which are potential eggs, and every month, on average, one ovary releases an egg that has the potential, if it meets the right sperm, to become fertilized and grow into a baby. Ovulation occurs randomly each month from either ovary. Sometimes ovulation takes place in the same ovary during many consecutive months, while other times it can switch from one to the other ovary. Women who have only one ovary are likely to ovulate each month from the same ovary. Sometimes more than one egg can be released, and if both eggs are fertilized, dizygotic (nonidentical or fraternal) twins can be created. The incidence of double ovulation is related to a woman's ethnicity, as well as to her age.

Although a woman is born with hundreds of thousands of follicles, this number quickly shrinks because each month up to twenty follicles begin the process of releasing an egg, though only one actually does and the rest are reabsorbed. By the time a woman is in her midfifties, she will run out of eggs and go into menopause.

The growth of the follicles is triggered when the ovary senses follicle-stimulating hormone (FSH), which is secreted by the pituitary gland. This secretion is triggered when the hypothalamus (in the brain) causes an increase in the secretion of gonadotropin-releasing hormone (GnRH), which in turn results from a drop in the level of the hormone estrogen.

When You Should Go to a Gynecologist

Assuming that you have or will soon have a gynecologist, when should you go to see this doctor? Visiting your Ob/Gyn is important for your health, not only when you have problems but also for preventive care to diagnose problems before they become apparent.

Every woman should see an Ob/Gyn at the latest when she turns eighteen or earlier if she starts having sex earlier. Becoming sexually active introduces changes to your genitalia, so you want to be checked out to make sure that once you begin having sex, everything is okay. You can also discuss contraception to make sure you get pregnant only when you want to. In addition, you can discuss the prevention of sexually transmitted diseases or other concerns you may have about sex.

Mothers need to send their daughters to see a gynecologist way before they're considering having sex. Imagine that you're an eighteen- (or seventeen- or sixteen-) year-old girl, you have a boyfriend you've been seeing for six months, and you're thinking and worrying and fantasizing nonstop about whether it's the right time to have sex with him. How likely is it that part of your planning will include seeing a gynecologist? It's not likely that a daughter will advertise the fact that she's about to have sex. Mothers should simply assume that this day will come and, rather than adopting the attitude that sending her daughter to the gynecologist is like giving her the okay to have sex, look at it as a precaution that could save her daughter a lot of grief.

The Top Five Reasons to See an Ob/Gyn

1. The first time you have sex or when you reach the age of eighteen
2. When you're planning to get pregnant
3. When you think you could be pregnant
4. Anytime you have a complaint, including but not limited to the following:
   a. Irregular or absent menstrual periods
   b. Vaginal bleeding or spotting in between periods

    c. Lower abdominal pain, with or without intercourse

    d. Bloated abdomen

    e. Vaginal discharge (especially if it smells)

5. To have routine yearly preventive gynecological care, a breast examination, and a Pap smear

To begin with, if you notice any kind of a change in your lower abdomen, including your vagina, or you feel something unusual in your breasts, then don't wait to pick up the phone to make an appointment. What do I mean by change? The previous list covers some of the common reasons to see your Ob/Gyn.

One change would be a vaginal discharge, especially if it smells, or if you experience lower abdominal pain with or without intercourse, or your sexual partner has discovered that your vagina smells or tastes different than it did before. Any indication that everything doesn't seem right "down below" should lead you to make an appointment. Sometimes a particular symptom doesn't mean anything at all or at least doesn't require any treatment. On the other hand, though, a symptom you have today could be a sign of something more serious, even if it goes away. When some people get genital herpes, they get a full-blown attack that is very visible and very painful, but others may have only one tiny pimple (and some people don't exhibit any signs). So let's say you discover some change or a sore spot on your vagina, and you recently had sex with a new partner. Because it could be a sign of a sexually transmitted disease, you need to have it checked by a doctor. Why? Because it could disappear and never reappear, yet you would still have caught herpes and would still be capable of passing the disease on to other partners. (More about this later, but in brief, you could be shedding viruses that you can't see.) Would you want to be responsible for giving herpes to others? Of course not, so even this small sore spot is something that needs to be examined by a doctor.

I don't want to be an alarmist or turn you into a hypochondriac. Most of the time, a pimple is just a pimple, or a vaginal discharge is a simple change in your body—but only your doctor can tell that for sure. So although you may find yourself visiting the gynecologist and feeling foolish because your reason for going turns out to be trivial, don't feel that way. Here are two things to remember. First, your gynecologist won't think of you as being silly or a hypochondriac. Your gynecologist has seen countless cases where a symptom that seemed trivial was an early sign of something that was actually quite dangerous. All doctors have that "better to be safe than sorry" attitude. The other thing is, if you have a potentially serious condition, in most cases the earlier you catch it, the better the ultimate results. In some cases, if you can nip something in the bud, it won't be a serious problem at all, but if you wait one, two, six months, or longer, it could cause irreversible harm. And even if a cure is available, the odds are it will be a lot more onerous and costly.

I hope that as a result of this chapter, you will resolve to become a lot more familiar with your genitals. And you know what? They're worth it!

From Dr. Amos's Office: Sally's Story

One of my patients who was trying to get pregnant noticed that she had some irregular bleeding in between her periods, and she immediately made an appointment to see me. I examined her and ordered some tests that showed a small growth inside her uterus. We performed a minor surgical procedure to remove the growth, and it turned out to be a benign polyp of the uterine lining. Had she waited much longer to have it removed, the polyp may have grown more, the bleeding could have become worse, and she might have needed a more complicated surgery. Or it could have interfered with her ability to get pregnant. Calling your doctor early when you have symptoms may prevent more complications in the future.

3

All about Your Monthly Cycle

No woman likes having a monthly episode of bleeding, better known as her menstrual period, but we don't have much of a choice. In this chapter you'll discover why menstruation happens, and that might make you feel a little better the next time you get your monthly visit.

When you were born, there were several million eggs located in your ovaries. These immature eggs are called follicles. As you grew older, many of the follicles died off, and by the time you entered puberty, there were only about four hundred thousand of them left. Each month, one of these becomes an actual egg and gets released from one of your ovaries in the hopes of meeting a sperm and becoming fertilized. Each month another thousand or so follicles die so that by the time you hit your late forties, not many are left. Around that time, your ovulation and your monthly cycle will change and eventually stop, and that's called menopause.

The exact age that this occurs is slightly different for every woman, but the median age is fifty-two.

Each month one of your ovaries (you have two) releases an egg, which goes down the fallopian tubes, the likely location for the egg to meet a sperm and become fertilized. If this particular egg gets lucky, then pregnancy will occur (more about that in chapter 8). But if there are no sperm awaiting the egg, it will continue its journey down the tube and finally die. This is the norm, because most women go through only a small number of pregnancies during their lifetimes, and the dissolution of the egg will trigger their period.

Had the egg been fertilized, it would have implanted itself into the wall of your uterus (assuming all was going well), and as it grew into a baby, it would have needed to draw nourishment. Your uterus prepared itself for this eventuality by building a blood supply. If no fertilized egg implants itself, though, the blood supply is not needed, and the blood detaches from the walls of the uterus and flows through the cervix and out of your vagina. That blood flow is part of your monthly menstrual period.

Day 1 of your cycle is the first day of your period, when the blood first starts to flow. From day 1 until ovulation happens is called the follicular phase. Once your old uterine lining has been shed, your uterus will begin the process of rethickening, preparing itself for the next possible fertilized egg. On day 1, your hormones estrogen and progesterone are at their lowest levels, but they slowly start to build. This phase normally lasts between seven and twenty-one days until ovulation next occurs.

The day you ovulate is the beginning of the second phase of your monthly cycle, called the luteal phase, because an increase in the luteinizing hormone kicks off the process that will cause the release of an egg about twenty-four hours later. Your levels of progesterone will rise as the endometrial lining of your uterus builds back up in preparation for the next potential fertilized egg.

Although this entire cycle is supposed to take, on average, twenty-eight days, not every woman has an actual twenty-eight-day cycle and not every woman is regular, meaning that her cycles may vary in length from month to month. The length of the menstrual cycle depends on the day of ovulation, which can vary from day 7 to day 21. When you add fourteen days for the luteal phase, a normal cycle (consisting of a follicular and a luteal phase) can last between twenty-one and thirty-five days.

There are women, some for religious reasons, who rely on their monthly cycles to predict which days of the month they are likely to be fertile (meaning that an egg is in the fallopian tubes, ready to meet a sperm), so to prevent an unintended pregnancy, they will avoid sex on those days. As you just read, though, not every woman has a regular cycle that can be predicted, mostly because ovulation happens on different days, and even those who do may go off schedule from time to time for a variety of reasons (including stress). So this method of birth control is highly unreliable, and if you don't wish to have an unintended pregnancy, I strongly suggest that you use another method of contraception.

Painful Periods

Although it's far from uncommon for a woman to feel some pain during the first few days of her period, if the pain is so bad that she cannot function normally, it's called dysmenorrhea. Usually, younger women complain of pain the most often, and if their becoming a few years older doesn't cause the pain to lessen, often getting pregnant will. Yet some women never completely grow out of these painful episodes.

For a very long time, women who complained of this pain were told it was all in their heads, but now the science of medicine knows what causes this pain, and it's most certainly not psychological (though there might be a psychological component if a woman feels that she is going to experience pain, because this will sensitize her to it, thus making any painful sensations feel that much worse).

The main cause of this pain is an excessive production of prostaglandins. These hormones stimulate the walls of your uterus to contract, thus helping the process by which the lining sloughs off and exits via your period. If you have too much of this hormone, then the necessary muscle contractions turn into painful cramping.

Some women experience pain before their menses begin, and it lasts for quite a long time. Although the "normal" cramping is called primary dysmenorrhea, this other type is labeled secondary dysmenorrhea. It can have many causes, including endometriosis, which means that tissue similar to the lining of your uterus is located outside of the uterus, or fibroids, which can grow in the uterus or in other parts of the reproductive system. If your doctor suspects that endometriosis is the cause, he or she will conduct tests. See chapter 5 for more information.

The remedies for such cramping include taking a nonsteroidal anti-inflammatory drug such as ibuprofen (Motrin or Advil), taking birth control pills (which is something you should discuss with your doctor), taking vitamin B1 or magnesium supplements, massage, acupuncture or acupressure, applying heat to the area via a warm bath or a heating pad, practicing yoga or meditation, or even having sex, because some women report that orgasms relieve their symptoms.

Another cause of dysmenorrhea is a medical condition called endometriosis. Talk to your doctor if you want to make sure endometriosis is excluded as a cause for painful periods.

By the way, I was quite surprised to learn that one of the methods to relieve pain offered by the American Congress of Obstetrics and Gynecologists was to have sex. Now, I am all for relieving pain, and I am all for having sex, but somehow it doesn't sit right with me to combine the two. Having sex as a pain reliever will put pressure on both partners. What if the woman doesn't have an orgasm? What if the pain prevents her from having an orgasm? What if he's not in the mood? What if she has an orgasm, and she's still in pain?

If two partners want to have sex, and it so happens that she's having some menstrual cramps, and afterward these are relieved, then I say, great. If from time to time when she's having cramps, she actually plans to have sex as a method of relieving her pain, I can even accept that. But sex isn't like a bottle of aspirin, and I would suggest that on a long-term basis, women don't rely on this particular method of relieving menstrual pain. If a woman discovers that orgasms are really a source of pain relief, then I would encourage her to masturbate, rather than use her sexual relationship as a means to that end.

Heavy Bleeding

The first time you had your period, you were undoubtedly nervous. Hopefully, your mother told you to expect it, but nevertheless, having blood come out of your vagina and in quantities that might seem serious is not an experience that you can completely prepare yourself for. After a while, though, you got used to this monthly visit and the amount of blood. Yet there might come a time when a noticeable increase in blood occurs (the medical term is menorrhagia), or you might wonder whether the amount of blood you lose every month is normal. How do you tell if you are bleeding heavily?

One way would be to weigh your tampons or pads. "Heavy" bleeding would be indicated by more than four to five ounces of blood in each period. But if that's a bit complicated and, shall we say, "icky," an easier, if less scientific, measure would be to see if you have to change your tampon or pad because it's soaked every hour for twenty-four hours. If that's the case, then you're bleeding heavily. (Another scale some women use is if they have to change their tampons or pads every half hour for six hours.)

There are many possible reasons for heavy menstrual periods, including ovulation issues and hormonal imbalance, uterine fibroids, a condition called adenomyosis, certain pregnancy complications

From Dr. Amos's Office: Debra's Story

A nineteen-year-old patient came to see me because she felt that her periods were too heavy, and she worried because there were some clots. She was using two to three tampons a day for two or three days, then one tampon a day for the next two days. I explained that it is normal to use two to three tampons a day, and often she would notice little clots as well as blood in her period. It's nothing to be alarmed about; it's just part of the lining of the endometrium and perfectly normal. The color of the blood that comes from a woman's period may also vary from red to brown, and that shouldn't be cause for alarm either.

As part of my recommendations, I asked her to keep a diary of her menstrual bleeding. She e-mailed me the diary three months later, and it showed that she was bleeding every fifteen days for five days. The time between the first day of menstrual bleeding or period until the first day of the next bleeding is called the menstrual cycle, and her cycle was fifteen days. A normal menstrual cycle lasts twenty-one to thirty-five days, with an average of twenty-eight to twenty-nine days. Very short cycles usually mean there is a problem with ovulation. Had she wanted to become pregnant, I would have done some tests and given her medication to induce ovulation. Because she did not want to become pregnant, I gave her birth control pills, which regulated her bleeding.

such as having a miscarriage, coagulation and blood problems, an intrauterine device, and polyps, as well as some cancers.

Because any of these could be the culprit and would require medical treatment, if you have an episode of very heavy vaginal bleeding that lasts for many days, call your doctor's office and make an appointment to see your gynecologist. Of course, if you are bleeding very heavily, the blood is bright red, and you feel weak, then go to the nearest emergency room. Even if it's not serious, it's better to let a doctor tell you this than to guess. Potentially heavy bleeding could signify a ruptured blood vessel, and then you could bleed to death. Another potential consequence of heavy bleeding could be anemia, in which case your doctor may prescribe that you take supplements, including iron.

Your doctor's first step is to try find out the cause for the heavy bleeding. Tests may include ultrasounds, a hysteroscopy to look inside the uterus, a biopsy, and some blood tests. Treatments are different, depending on the cause of the bleeding. Sometimes your doctor will give you hormones to stop the bleeding; other times there are surgical methods, such as a D&C (dilation and curettage) and even a hysterectomy (removal of the uterus). Again, whether one of these methods is right for you is something to discuss with your doctor.

Amenorrhea

A complete cessation of your period is called amenorrhea.

Primary amenorrhea is diagnosed when you have had no menstrual period by age sixteen, and secondary amenorrhea is diagnosed when you haven't had a period for three months, although some physicians make that diagnosis at less than three months.

There are three main causes of having secondary amenorrhea:

1. Pregnancy is a major reason for missing periods in sexually active women, especially if they don't use contraception. So, first you need a pregnancy test to find out if that's what is causing your lack of periods.
2. If you are approaching menopause, then this is the likely cause of your amenorrhea, although you should still consult with your physician.
3. Not ovulating, which is called anovulation. The main cause of anovulation is polycystic ovarian syndrome. Other reasons for not ovulating include breast-feeding, stress, taking contraceptives, low body weight, thyroid disease, ovarian failure, and certain medications.

Primary amenorrhea is rare and happens in fewer than one in a hundred women. The causes include problems with a small gland in the brain, the hypothalamus; chromosome issues; and abnormalities of the vagina and the uterus.

Many women who are breast-feeding count on that fact to protect them from another pregnancy. While it is true that breast-feeding will prevent ovulation for a certain amount of time, it's not permanent and at most will delay ovulation only slightly. Because you'll have no warning that you've ovulated, relying on the fact that you're breast-feeding as a method of birth control is especially unreliable.

Women who have eating disorders or who do a lot of aerobic exercise often experience amenorrhea. In both cases, the level of body fat in these women is very low, and because the hormone estrogen is manufactured by body fat, this can cause a woman to have fewer or no periods, which in turn means she is not ovulating. This can have long-term consequences, including osteoporosis, so she would need to talk over this condition with a doctor.

The medical conditions that can cause amenorrhea include a malfunction in the thyroid, which controls the release of an

---

From Dr. Amos's Office: Natalie's Story

During a regular yearly checkup, my patient told me she had not had a period for four months. Apparently, this happened regularly, and she was not concerned. I did a sonogram, and it showed an eight-week pregnancy. She eventually went on to have a healthy baby girl. This example shows that even though you are used to not getting a period and may not have had one for some time, you can still get pregnant. Pregnancy can happen any time you ovulate, and ovulation can occur even if you have not had a period for a while. Your menstrual period follows ovulation (if you are not pregnant), so even when you don't get your period, you must use birth control for contraception if you do not want to get pregnant.

important hormone that triggers your period, prolactin. Prolactin is manufactured in your pituitary gland, so amenorrhea could indicate a problem with that gland. Certain women develop scarring of the uterus, which can also cause them to cease menstruating. Although some women might welcome a cessation of their menses, the underlying cause may signify a health issue, such as those described previously, so it needs to be diagnosed and treated by their gynecologist.

Toxic Shock Syndrome

Toxic shock syndrome (TSS) is a serious but rare disease, which for a short time blossomed in the early 1970s and was traced to the use of a brand of superabsorbent tampons that has since been taken off the market. This tampon absorbed not only the menstrual blood but also all of the vaginal fluids, which led to damage of the vaginal walls and in turn allowed the bacteria that cause TSS (which are normally on your skin and are harmless) to enter the bloodstream, where they can turn deadly.

The risks of getting TSS are very small these days, but if you want to lower the risk even more, either don't use highly absorbent tampons or limit their use to the days when your period is at its heaviest and use pads at night. Also, never use high-absorbent tampons for more than two days in a row.

4

Getting the Most Out of Your Visit to the Gynecologist

I'm going to let you in on a little secret: if you want the best health care, it is vital that you provide your doctor with the highest quality information. Because doctors are always prodding and poking you, taking various measurements, and so forth, you might think that they can get all they need to know without much involvement on your part. Yet like anything else, the more you put into something, the more you'll get out of it, and I'll show you how. In addition, I'll also discuss that all-important question: whether your gynecologist should be male or female.

In this chapter, you'll find a topic that you've probably never thought about: taking your medical history. This process is not limited to a visit to the gynecologist, and because you've done it so many times before, you might be tempted to skip this chapter, but please don't. If you were building a house, you wouldn't decide that it didn't need a foundation. Your medical history is the foundation of all of your medical care. Dr. Amos and I think it is important enough that we've dedicated an entire chapter to this subject, and we hope you'll give it the attention it deserves.

From Dr. Amos's Office: Amy's Story

A woman came to see me in my New York office. She was using birth control, had recently moved to New York from Chicago, and was thinking of stopping birth control and trying to have another baby. This type of consultation is called periconception counseling, in which someone sees a doctor before becoming pregnant, to find out how to improve her chances of having a healthier pregnancy.

Among the many questions I asked her was one about her previous pregnancy. Her first child was three years old. I asked her about the delivery, and she said that her son had weighed more than 10 pounds at birth, so he had to be delivered by Cesarean section after she had been in a long labor. She asked me whether she'd need another C-section or could she deliver vaginally, but after hearing her story and seeing her physical stature (she was 5 feet 7 inches tall and weighed 190 pounds), I immediately had several concerns.

Overweight babies are often born to mothers who have diabetes, so her overweight baby could be a sign that she had diabetes. The first thing I did was order a glucose challenge blood test, which is conducted one hour after the mother ingests 75 grams of a glucose solution. Sure enough, she did have elevated sugar levels in her bloodstream and was a diabetic. Diabetes is a silent disease, at least in the beginning, and many people unknowingly have it without experiencing special symptoms. It's often at the advanced stage, when organs are already damaged, that people realize they have diabetes. We discussed postponing pregnancy and starting treatment, which included her making dietary changes, seeing a nutritionist, exercising, and losing weight before pregnancy. She came back three months later, having lost 24 pounds, and with her diabetic diet and healthier weight I gave her a green light to get pregnant. Ten months later, she delivered a healthy 7 pound, 8 ounce, baby girl.

The woman in the previous case went to the gynecologist with one question but ended up discovering a medical problem that she had no clue about. This is why it's so important to discuss your entire medical history with your doctor during all visits but especially before you try to get pregnant. Your doctor needs to see the entire picture and from that can often deduce medical issues that you had never considered.

The next step you would take after being diagnosed with diabetes or prediabetes is to change your lifestyle, and in this instance your doctor can be an important ally. It's one thing to go on a diet to lose weight to improve your appearance. It's entirely a different matter when you decide to follow a healthier diet to avoid getting a disease as severe as diabetes. Not only are you more likely to listen to your doctor's orders, but so will everyone else around you. For example, if a friend offers you some candy, and you simply say, "No, thanks," that friend is more likely to push you into having a piece. Because of that pressure, you might take one or two. Yet if you say, "No, thanks, my doctor told me to avoid sweets," then your friend will put away the candy without another word. In such instances, your doctor becomes an invisible ally, and all of this results from him or her having access to your comprehensive medical history.

Some women look at their gynecologist as the doctor who deals only with their reproductive systems, but the truth is that an obstetrician/gynecologist can also be a woman's primary care doctor. This means you don't have to go to two doctors but can use your gynecologist as your main doctor. If you have a problem that is beyond your gynecologist's ability to handle, you'll be referred to a specialist, but that's true of any primary care physician—that is, family doctor—that you might see.

There's another advantage in using your gynecologist as your primary care doctor. Many women feel nervous about undergoing a pelvic exam, but women who use their gynecologists as primary care physicians feel a lot less nervous about it. That makes sense because the better the relationship you have with your gynecologist, the more confidence you'll have in him or her and the less tense you'll be in the stirrups.

By the way, don't think that you're the only one to be nervous about getting a pelvic exam. While researching this book, I spoke to a group of nurses who work for obstetricians and gynecologists at the New York Weill Cornell Medical Center. These nurses are very involved in the practice of gynecology and spend their days giving advice to patients, yet they admitted that when they have to go for a gynecological exam, they feel anxious, too. Sure, some of that anxiety would occur with any medical exam because it could lead to a diagnosis of an illness, but their anxiety was also due to the nature of what takes place in the examining room. (If you learn nothing else from this book, at least you now know that the nurses at your gynecologist's office sympathize with you, no matter how stern their outer appearance might be, because they feel very similar to the way you do.) If these well-trained nurses also feel uncomfortable undergoing this process, you certainly have nothing to be ashamed of.

No matter how well you know your gynecologist, it may be impossible to eliminate all feelings of apprehension, because any time we humans enter a situation that produces anxiety, our bodies go into what is called the fight-or-flight state. This means that your body begins to produce extra adrenaline to get you ready to either flee or fight this danger. Of course, in this situation you're voluntarily at the doctor's office and are not going to fight or run away, but these added chemicals coursing through your bloodstream will affect your mental state, and you cannot completely alleviate the stress. The best you can do is understand it and try to calm yourself down by telling yourself there's really nothing to fear.

Whether or not your gynecologist is your primary care physician, for the medical history part of the exam to be most effective, you have to be completely honest. If your doctor asks if you smoke, and you do, then you have to admit it. The same is true with drinking alcohol and even taking illegal drugs. Your doctor will not turn you in (even in court, the doctor-patient relationship remains confidential).

It is very important for gynecologists to know whether you've had any sexually transmitted diseases, especially if you're pregnant. Although you may prefer to keep your sex life private, it's essential that you not hide your sexual history from your doctor. Anything that might put you at risk—and that's for your doctor to decide, not you—must be revealed to your doctor. Not being honest when answering your doctor's questions is never to your advantage.

Knowing that your doctor will ask about your family's medical history may force you to prepare by doing some research. You may not be familiar with how most of your relatives passed away, for example, but that's something your doctor will want to know about. You may have to ask your living relatives how your extended family members died. Maybe one side of your family lives across

From Dr. Amos's Office: Helen's Story

A woman came to see me who had already suffered three miscarriages and was concerned about her ability to bear a child. As I took her medical history, she revealed that her mother had died of a stroke. I asked whether anyone else in her family had any similar problems. She said that her aunt had died ten years ago, but she wasn't sure of the cause. I asked her to check, and it turned out to be from a blood clot in her lungs. It was beginning to look as if there might be a genetic trait in her family for this type of problem, and because having miscarriages was also a sign, I ordered her to go for some blood tests. Sure enough, she had a genetic predisposition toward developing blood clots, which can lead to strokes and other complications, including those in pregnancy. This condition is especially dangerous during pregnancy because it can lead not only to miscarriages but also to a life-threatening condition called preeclampsia. For her next pregnancy, which was considered high-risk, she would need to start treatment early on and be watched very closely until delivery.

the country, and you simply don't know them very well. If that's the case, you have to find out whether they have any serious conditions that run on that side of the family because it would mean that you might be more liable to develop this condition. If your doctor knows that a certain disease is in your gene pool, he or she will look more carefully for early signs of this disease in you.

Because I have only one living relative, an uncle, I have no idea what genetic predispositions I may have. If you have a family, don't ignore this important resource but instead make sure to learn as much about your family as possible, including any health issues they may have.

Now that you have an overall view of why it is important to answer your doctor's questions fully and honestly, let's get more specific about all of the topics that will be raised.

Allergies

Although you may think of an allergy as something that makes your nose run, the most important allergies, from your doctor's point of view, are any that you might have to drugs. Keep in mind that feeling nauseated or dizzy after taking a medicine is not generally considered an allergy. I am not talking about simply sneezing or having an itchy nose, ears, or throat. A serious allergy usually manifests as skin eruptions such as hives, a swollen throat, shortness of breath, low blood pressure, or even shock. If you've ever had such an allergic reaction to something you ingested, to any drug, to an antibiotic such as penicillin, for example, or even to an over-the-counter medication such as aspirin, you must tell your doctor. Even if your doctor is prescribing another drug and not the one you are known to be allergic to, this drug can sometimes cause an allergic reaction if it shares certain similarities with one you are allergic to. This is not a question for you to decide but for your doctor, and the only way your doctor will be able to make an informed decision is if he or she knows of every possible allergic reaction you've had in your life.

While your doctor is most concerned about any allergies you have to drugs, it's also important for him or her to know about all of your allergies, such as to pollen, nuts, and so on. People who have some allergies are more prone to other allergies, so a full knowledge of your allergies will be a factor in the decisions your doctor makes about your care.

Current Medications

Your doctor needs to know whether you are currently taking any medications, including those that do not require a prescription, the so-called over-the-counter medications, such as aspirin, or even herbal remedies and vitamins. Your doctor may also want to know, for example, if you had some joint pain two weeks ago and took a painkiller. Yet even more important are drugs that you take regularly, whether they are by prescription or over the counter. For example, some people take low-dose aspirin on a daily basis because they've heard it can prevent heart disease. Aspirin is a blood thinner, though, and if you were going to be operated on, it would be essential that you stop taking aspirin, even if it's a low

---

From Dr. Amos's Office: Joanne's Story

During the first visit of her pregnancy, my patient denied that she took any medications. When I asked her whether she took supplements, she mentioned taking an herbal supplement called kava-kava to reduce anxiety symptoms. I explained to her that there are no studies showing that kava-kava is safe to use in pregnancy, and that some doctors are actually concerned that it may not be safe. My patient was surprised and said she thought all herbs were safe. She stopped taking kava-kava and, after a pregnancy with no complications, delivered a healthy baby. This example shows that it's important to discuss with your doctor all of the supplements you take, even vitamins, because some may not be considered safe during pregnancy.

dose, for several days ahead of the surgery. Don't assume that you can decide which medications you should reveal and which you needn't bother to mention. Your doctor doesn't need to know that you take cough drops to relieve a tickle, but remember to bring up the other pills and medications, including over-the-counter vitamins and herbal products, because any or all of them could have an effect that your doctor needs to know about.

Your Medical and Physical History

Although I hope that you've had a lifetime of good health, many people have experienced either a serious medical condition or accident somewhere along the way. Even if you're not going to a particular doctor for that condition, it's very important that you tell any doctor who treats you about your full medical history. For example, when you visit the gynecologist, you will have your blood pressure taken. Certain people's blood pressure becomes elevated when they're at the doctor's office because they're nervous, so in this case a slightly elevated blood pressure might not be significant.

One way to avoid this elevated blood pressure, however, is to rest on your side for a little while before your blood pressure is taken. If a nurse asks to take your blood pressure while you are standing up or right after you enter the room, make sure to request that it not be taken until you have rested on your side, lying down.

Of course, if you have a history of high blood pressure, that's something the doctor needs to know about. If it's your first visit to this particular doctor, simply the fact that you've had your blood pressure taken might not give the doctor enough information, and blood pressure is only one of many, many factors. But if you tell your doctor about your past medical history, that will give him or her a valuable tool when diagnosing whatever findings are derived from this particular examination.

It is especially important to let your doctor know of any vaginal infections you have had. Sometimes frequent yeast infections are associated with certain medical conditions such as diabetes, which is why your doctor should be told about them so that he or she can examine you further. Vaginal discharge and infections could also come from sexually transmitted diseases, which your doctor can check for, but this will take place only if you let him or her know about these symptoms. Infections can also lead to a preterm birth, and knowing about them and treating them can prevent this from happening. If your doctor knows to look for infections and possibly screen for them, then this risk may be avoided. But if you fail to tell your doctor, he or she won't assume anything, and then you could develop an infection later on that will cause complications.

Although you might think you don't need to reveal psychological issues to your doctor, you should definitely mention them. Here again, let me offer an example. If you complain to your gynecologist that it's difficult for you to have an orgasm and you've been diagnosed with depression, this is very significant. Your depressed state could cause your doctor to change his or her advice. If you are on any type of medication for depression, this is also important to reveal. Certain medications can have side effects that affect sexual functioning, which your doctor will be aware of. If you don't want to tell your doctor about a psychological problem, you might be tempted to skip any mention of drugs you are on, because they would reveal that you do have a psychological issue. This would only be counterproductive, however, so it's better to be completely open in such cases, even though your gynecologist will not treat you for depression.

Part of your psychological well-being depends on the state of your intimate relationship. If you and your partner are not getting along, that will cause extra stress. It might also be an important reason for you not to become pregnant until you feel better. Plenty of couples whose relationships are in tatters still have sex. If they were to end up having an unintended pregnancy, it would truly complicate matters. You may feel that your doctor doesn't need to know about your relationship with your significant other, but if the relationship could have a present or future negative effect on your health, then you should consider your doctor an ally and let him or her know what's going on in your life.

Your doctor will also want information about any accidents you may have had that left a serious impact. Why is it important for your gynecologist to know that you broke your leg skiing ten years ago? First of all, you may have sustained an internal injury that wasn't discovered but that might play a role in a problem you have now. Or if you walk slightly differently than you should, the doctor will want to know the reason for this; otherwise, he or she might start looking for another cause.

Your doctor needs to know which immunizations you've had. If you didn't have a standard immunization, that could put your future children at risk if you were to contract a disease while pregnant, so it's important that this information be on your chart to enable your doctor to take extra care if you do become pregnant.

Your gynecologist will also need to know everything about your reproductive status. This would include the date of your last period, whether your menstrual cycles are regular, when your last visit to the gynecologist was and what tests were done and the results, and any pregnancies that you underwent, whether or not they came to term (of course, if you are seeing your regular gynecologist, all of this information will already be in your chart).

You should tell your doctor your marital status and, if you're single, whether you're sexually active and with how many partners. Doctors also usually want to know whether you are in a hetero-sexual or a same-sex relationship, because each can be associated with different health conditions. This is important information for your doctor because if you have multiple sexual partners, it increases the risk of your catching a sexually transmitted disease.

From Dr. Amos's Office: Katie's Story

One of my patients came to me for her routine yearly examination. I had delivered her twin girls six years earlier, and she had been married for more than ten years. Her Pap test showed an infection, and I did laboratory tests for sexually transmitted diseases, which came back positive for chlamydia. I gave her a treatment for herself and her husband and repeated the tests six months later. She was again positive for chlamydia. It turned out that her husband had been having an affair with another woman, who infected him and in turn he infected his wife.

Even if you have only one sexual partner, your partner may have multiple sexual partners, and this can increase your chances of getting a sexually transmitted disease.

In this case, during the examination, the doctor will want to look for any potential signs that you might be infected.

You'll also be asked about your place of work. Remember, your gynecologist is responsible for your overall health, so if you work in an environment that exposes you to pollutants or other factors that could have a negative impact on your health, your doctor will want to check whether they have in fact caused you any harm. Definitely don't forget to tell your doctor if your job is particularly stressful. Stress can impair your health in many ways, especially if you are having difficulties becoming pregnant. Your job may affect you not only physically but psychologically as well. You should report any stressful situation, not only job-related ones. If you have a sick parent, for example, and that is causing you a lot of worry and perhaps requiring nightly visits to a hospital, this situation will have just as much of an effect on your health as any job-related stress.

So far, I've dealt with all of the negatives in your life that could affect your health, but don't be shy about reporting any positive information. If you exercise regularly or are careful about what you eat, tell your doctor. For example, if you run marathons, then your heart will be stronger than normal and will therefore beat slower when you're not running. It would be important for your doctor to know this, or else he or she might wonder why your heartbeat is so slow. Or, if you are very careful about what you eat, yet nevertheless have slightly elevated sugar levels, your doctor might be more concerned because it could indicate prediabetes.

You know that your doctor is very busy and is not supposed to act as your psychologist, so you may tend not to bother the doctor with too many details about your life. Yet although a gynecologist is often not there to provide a shoulder to cry on, I hope the examples in this chapter show that it's preferable to give him or her more information, even too much information, rather than hold back.

Revealing certain personal information may have an immediate effect on you; for example, you might start to cry. So you may be tempted not to confide something painful in order to keep your emotions in check. Although that's appropriate in most circumstances, it's not the best tactic in the doctor's office. It's very important that you provide your doctor with the full picture. If you hold back to keep from crying or appearing weak or for any other reason, your doctor won't be able to give you the best care.

From Dr. Amos's Office: Maria's Story

One of my patients came to see me for a routine examination. She had no complaints, and when I asked about her previous sexual partners, she confided that she'd had a boyfriend just prior to meeting her husband and that the old boyfriend just told her that he had been treated for a sexually transmitted disease shortly after they broke up. I tested her, and she was positive. Treating my patient and her husband successfully cured her condition. This example shows that it is important to talk to your doctor about everything that may affect your health, even if on the surface it does not seem relevant.

The Top Ten Pieces of Personal Information about You and Your Partner That Your Doctor Needs to Know

1. Your family and genetic history
2. Your daily life and environment
3. Your diet and eating habits
4. Prior fertility issues
5. Pregnancy history
6. Gynecological issues
7. Infections
8. Prior medical history
9. Prior surgical history
10. Over-the-counter and prescription medications

Choosing Your Physician

Whether you're going to cry or reveal all that you should will depend a lot on the relationship you have with your doctor, so a key requirement in getting the best medical care is choosing the right physician. The most basic question you have to ask is whether you need a doctor who is only a gynecologist or one who is also an obstetrician. If you're of child-bearing age, unless you've decided not to have children, then you're probably better off having a gynecologist who is also an obstetrician. There certainly may be exceptions to that, but if you're planning to look for a doctor, you might as well find one who can also deliver your baby.

Many doctors go beyond the standard training to become board certified. For gynecologists, this means they have been certified by the American Board of Obstetrics and Gynecology, and they become fellows of the American College of Obstetricians and Gynecologists, or ACOG. Yet that is not where their education stops. Board-certified Ob/Gyns need to continue with regular education and recertification in order to maintain their certificates. Dr. Amos and I recommend that whenever possible, you seek out a board-certified obstetrician and gynecologist because that ensures you are seeing a doctor with the highest level of qualifications.

There was a time, not so long ago, when finding a female doctor of any sort was a rarity. That's not true anymore, because more and more women are choosing to become doctors and especially gynecologists. It does make sense that some women would prefer to have a female gynecologist. After all, a female doctor will not only have studied what it's like to menstruate, for example, but will have experienced it, too. Yet it's not always the right decision, and I'm not saying this because my coauthor, a male gynecologist, is looking over my shoulder! First of all, some women actually have an easier time with a male physician, psychologically speaking. Choosing a doctor is a very personal decision that only you, the patient, can make, and gender may be only one of many variables that you will consider. Just because a doctor is a woman does not necessarily make her more qualified, and she is not automatically "warm and fuzzy." Some of the nurses I spoke with said that they much prefer a male gynecologist, because they have an easier time talking to a male doctor than to a female.

The bottom line is that whether you decide on a female or a male gynecologist should depend on how you feel and on the skills and the approach of the individual doctor. If you live in a big city that offers a wide choice of doctors, and if you really prefer a female to examine you and answer your questions, then by all means you should look for a female gynecologist. If, however, you live in a region where the selection of gynecologists is more limited or your choice of doctors is artificially restricted by your insurance company, then I suggest that you judge your doctors by their competence and manner first; their gender should play only a minor role in your decision.

Preparing for Your Visit to the Gynecologist

It's important to learn how to maximize a visit to the gynecologist. These days, you can't afford not to get the most out of every visit to the doctor. Here are some tips that will address your concerns and help you prepare.

Many women find the physical examination by a gynecologist anxiety-producing. That's not true for everyone, though. Some women don't consider the exam a big deal. Hopefully, after you read this book, you'll be closer to that attitude. It isn't surprising that some women may be uncomfortable with the idea of a gynecological exam. When you were a little girl, your mother always reminded you that if you were wearing a dress or a skirt, no one should catch a glimpse of even your underwear. At first, you might not have gotten the message, because at age two or three you really didn't care. Yet eventually it sank in and became embedded into your psyche that the area between your legs was very, very private. Because of such attitudes, there are women who despite being in long-term sexual relationships remain very uncomfortable with showing their vaginas even to their partners. When having sexual relations, they insist on remaining either under the covers or in the dark. To those women, having their genitals examined under a bright light seems like a nightmare come true.

Would it help you to know that the doctor has seen thousands of naked women's genitalia, vaginas, and other private parts? This might enable some women to rationalize about what's going to happen, but let's be truthful here, it's not the doctor's problem, it's yours. Your anxiety isn't about what the doctor may feel during the exam but about how you're feeling. It's not about what he or she is looking at but instead what you're showing and how that makes you feel. That's why it really doesn't matter all that much if the doctor is a man or a woman. Chances are, you'd be no more likely to invite your neighbor to come look at your vagina if she was a woman than a man, and there are plenty of women who won't even look at their own vaginas in a mirror.

In case you skipped chapter 2, here's another pitch to convince you to look closely at your genitals. The more your vagina is a stranger to you, the more difficult it will be to show it to a doctor. Remember, this isn't about the doctor, it's about you. So if you get used to looking at your own vagina, you'll feel more relaxed about having it examined by a doctor during a pelvic exam.

This concept applies not only to a pelvic exam but also to having sex. The more comfortable you are with your own body, the more you'll enjoy having sex with a partner. The reverse is also true; the more uptight you are about your body, the less you'll be able to enjoy sex with a partner. Although it's a good idea to look at your vagina in a mirror to prepare for a pelvic exam, it's equally important to do this to improve your love life. If the former reason wasn't enough to get you to take a mirror and have a look around, then I hope the second one is!

By the way, some gynecologists may ask if you would like to use a mirror during the exam so that you can see what is taking place. Some women find it more comforting to watch the exam, and others feel that it would make them more nervous. The choice is yours. Use the mirror, look up at the ceiling, or even close your eyes. In any case, even if you start using the mirror to see what's happening, you can always set it aside if you find it easier not to look.

Let's talk about how you should prepare for a gynecological exam. Just as you are required not to eat anything starting at midnight the night before you go for blood tests, you can take certain steps to prepare for a trip to the gynecologist.

First, make a list of anything that you should inform your doctor about. If you are experiencing any current physical problems, such as urinary tract infections, unusual discharges, or pains of any sort (perhaps during intercourse), you must tell your doctor. You may think that these conditions or symptoms will be apparent, but they might not be. In any case, it will help the doctor if you report these before the exam begins. Your doctor will want to know when you had your last period, how long it lasted, and whether your periods are regular (including whether you have any bleeding between periods). If you're one of those women who gets surprised each month by the arrival of your period, make an effort to keep track of your cycle in the months before your exam.

Your Period

If you are having your period when you visit the gynecologist, the blood may make it more difficult for your doctor to clearly see the condition of your vagina. If you expect to have your menstrual period on the day of the doctor's appointment, you may want to call ahead and ask the doctor's office if it makes a difference and whether you should change your appointment to a different time. Of course, if you have a problem that requires the doctor's immediate attention and you're having your period, then don't worry about it and make the soonest possible appointment. Don't forget to let the nurse who makes the appointment know that you have an actual problem and that it's not simply a routine exam, so that she can schedule you in as soon as possible.

Sex

If at all possible, try not to have sex within a twenty-four- to forty-eight-hour period before your pelvic exam. If you must have sex, make your partner wear a condom. The presence of the ejaculate with sperm in the vagina may make it more difficult for your doctor to do certain examinations. If, for example, you have a vaginal discharge, it will be mixed in with semen (unless you used a condom), and that may interfere with the examination, so this is one reason not to have sex. The exam would be less effective, because the doctor would not get as clear a picture of your vagina's health. Yet as with any other aspect of preparing for a doctor's visit, if in doubt, call the office and find out what you can and cannot do.

Vaginal Condition

If you are using some sort of vaginal medication, don't apply it for twenty-four to forty-eight hours prior to your exam, whether it is over the counter or prescribed. It's better that the doctor be able to clearly see the condition of the problem you are treating, without the medication masking it to some degree. Regarding the regular use of douches or vaginal sprays to keep the vagina clean and smelling sweet (which most gynecologists frown on, by the way), you should not insert anything into your vagina, including tampons, for twenty-four to forty-eight hours before your exam. If it is an emergency visit, however, this rule does not apply.

If You've Ever Been Raped

Your gynecologist may ask if you've ever been raped. If you were and it happened a long time ago and you did not contract any sexually transmitted diseases, it probably will have no significant relevance to a current physical exam. Yet rape can have long-term psychological effects and could make you extra anxious during the exam. That's especially true if you underwent a pelvic exam right after the rape (which you should have, if you reported it to anyone). Therefore, subsequent pelvic exams could bring up memories of this very unpleasant experience. A doctor who does many such exams all day long can be a little insensitive at times. Yet any gynecologist who knows that he or she is treating a victim of rape will make an extra effort to keep you as calm as possible. As a result of rape, you can sometimes get infected with a sexually transmitted disease that needs to be treated, so let your doctor know if you've been a rape victim.

If you've ever been raped or molested in some way and still have psychological scars from that experience that affect not only a visit to the gynecologist but your romantic relationships as well, please go for counseling. You can get help, and there's no reason to suffer needlessly. You will never forget what happened, but that doesn't mean you should allow past events to harm you for the rest of your life.

Shaving

These days, many women shave some or all of their pubic hair. Certain women have been shaving their pubic hair because it is traditional in their society. The trend of shaving arose in part as oral sex became more prevalent, because a shaved vagina makes oral sex a bit more pleasant for a partner, although it's certainly not a necessity. Whether you choose to trim your hair to any degree is a personal decision. Does shaving (or any other form of hair removal) make it any easier for the gynecologist? The answer is absolutely not. Gynecologists don't care and don't think about it. This includes whether you shave your legs or remove any stray hairs on your breasts. So don't worry about the issue of hair, one way or another. Shaving your genitalia, on the other hand, can lead to an infection or other injuries in this area, so you need to take certain precautions before you shave your genital area.

Top Ten Tips from Dr. Amos on Shaving the Pubic Area

1. Buy a razor blade that is of good quality, and don't share it with anyone else.
2. Use a new razor or blade for each shave.
3. Try out any shaving cream you intend to use on a small area of your body to make sure you are not allergic to it.
4. Start by cutting your pubic hair shorter, using scissors that have a blunt tip to avoid accidentally injuring your skin.
5. Soak your pubic hair with lukewarm water first to make it softer, preferably in the shower.
6. Apply sufficient amounts of shaving cream to your pubic area.
7. Start shaving gently—it should not hurt.

8. Rinse the razor after several strokes to prevent hairs from accumulating and clogging it.

9. After you finish shaving, rinse the area carefully with warm water, then dry it with a clean towel.

10. Apply a soothing cream or some baby oil on the shaved area to keep it moisturized and protect it against skin irritation and itching.

Other Concerns

You're going to remove most, if not all, of your clothes for this exam, because the doctor will be looking at your breasts, as well as at your genital area and vagina. Your feet will be in stirrups right next to the doctor's face. What some women forget is that the gynecologist will be working between your legs, rather close to your elevated feet. If there's a smell emanating from this area, it will be embarrassing. Although you may needlessly worry about certain parts of your anatomy, the one area that you might concern yourself with is your feet. The doctor and the nurse will appreciate your concern as well. Some women even have a pedicure prior to their gynecological examinations, although that's not necessary.

If you don't want to show your feet, take some socks and wear them during the gynecological examination. The one article of clothing that you can leave on is socks, which will also protect your feet from cold floors. Just make sure that they smell fresh and have no holes.

The Pelvic Exam

Before I describe the exam, let's consider why your doctor needs to take such a close look at your vagina. Certainly, many men never have a doctor examine their penises the way a woman's vagina gets scrutinized so regularly. Why do women need to have this done? Understanding the reasons will make it a little easier for you to undergo the exam because you'll better appreciate why a doctor needs to peer between your legs.

One reason is that your vagina provides a "window" to the inside of your body. Doctors look into people's ears and noses and down their throats because there aren't very many spots on the human body where they can see what's happening below the surface of the skin. Doctors can diagnose certain conditions by looking inside your body that they can't by inspecting only the outside. For example, an ophthalmologist, an eye doctor, may detect that a patient has diabetes during an eye exam, long before a general practitioner discovers this disease in the patient. Because women can develop cancer of the cervix, and since a gynecologist can easily do a Pap test to check for cervical cancer, it makes sense that you should have this test done. Allowing the doctor to use this "window" into your body will help safeguard your health.

Another reason for a pelvic exam is that the vagina is a vessel, meaning that foreign objects, the male penis and the ejaculate, are regular visitors inside the vagina. Along with the elements of the ejaculate that are supposed to be there, such as the sperm, if any disease-carrying organisms are present, they, too, are carried into the vagina. Once they enter the vagina, they often don't simply stay there but move farther into the body, potentially infecting the uterus, the fallopian tubes, the ovaries, the blood, and other body parts. Not only do vaginas supply a window, they supply a front door through which women are very vulnerable. Having a doctor examine your vagina is therefore important to ensure that you are healthy.

Some of you who are reading this may ask, "But don't condoms offer protection from sexually transmitted diseases?" Condoms are effective against the transmission of most STDs, but they do not offer 100 percent protection against STDs or pregnancy. First of all, condoms can break or fall off, and sometimes they end up being used incorrectly or not used at all. During sex, by which I mean the entire act, not only intercourse, it's likely that the partner will place a finger or his tongue in the vagina, which is another manner of introducing disease-carrying microbes. This is one reason that doctors find women being infected with oral herpes in their genitals more often these days.

The vagina is a warm and moist place and is ideally suited for any microbes that manage to get inside to live and multiply. In addition, these microbes can travel to other parts of your body from the vagina. So it's important to make sure that if any of them do set up house, they get detected and evicted before they can do serious damage.

Don't forget that your vagina also plays an important role during sex. If it's not working properly, and that includes if you're having any difficulties achieving sexual satisfaction, this is also an issue that needs to be considered during the pelvic exam.

In most offices, you are required to first fill out a form about why you want to see your doctor and answer questions about your gynecological, medical, surgical, and social history. Oftentimes, the doctor will also meet you in his or her office to discuss your history and the reason for the visit.

A nurse will then bring you into an examination room. She will give you a gown and tell you to remove all of your clothes and put on the gown. Then she will leave the room. "All" means everything, except your socks. After you've undressed and donned your gown, you can sit on the examination table to await the doctor. (If this is your first exam, make sure that you tell the nurse. Then she'll know that you are extra nervous, and she may check back in with you more often if the doctor is delayed in starting the exam.)

During the actual exam, there will usually be a nurse or a chaperone inside the examining room the entire time that the exam is taking place. This is for your comfort so that you can have full confidence that the exam will be conducted in a professional manner. It's also for the doctor's protection for the same reason, because patients can sometimes act inappropriately. If you don't see a chaperone in the room, you may request one.

If you want to have a friend or a family member with you as well, most doctors won't object. That person will usually stand or sit near the top side of the table and will not be able to see anything that is going on during the exam, although if you decide to use a mirror, then the person might also be able to see what's taking place. On the other hand, if you don't mind, the doctor could show the other person anything "interesting" that becomes apparent.

On the examination table you'll place your feet in stirrups, which are metal objects that stick out. These stirrups usually fold away and probably won't be apparent while you're waiting for the doctor. The nurse will most likely pull the stirrups out when the doctor is ready to come in, and she'll ask you to place your feet in them, although if the doctor wants to talk to you first, that may not happen right away. Some examination rooms have metal stirrups that could be cold (hence the advantage of wearing socks), but others are covered in plastic. If you find the stirrups uncomfortable, ask that some padding be placed under the backs of your heels. This is a perfectly reasonable request; you should not have to experience any discomfort from having your feet in the stirrups.

The doctor will ask you to scoot your butt down to the very edge of the table. Having your genitals at the very edge of the table facilitates the doctor's job but also makes it more comfortable for you. Your knees will be up in the air because the stirrups are short, on purpose. If you have long legs and feel uncomfortable, ask your doctor to lengthen the stirrups so that your legs are a bit more extended.

You know how the dentist tells you to "Open wide"? Well, your gynecologist will need you to cooperate by spreading your legs widely. This will not be your first impulse, just as it doesn't feel normal to open wide for the dentist, but for the doctor to get in between your legs to get close to your vagina, you'll need to spread your legs.

The doctor may ask whether you want to hold a mirror with a long handle to see what is going on between your legs (some doctors even have video cameras to show you your genitalia on a screen). If you've taken my advice and have looked closely at your vagina with a mirror or a videocam on your own and understood what you were seeing, then you don't need to, unless you are curious to see what your cervix looks like, which you can't normally see on your own. Some women find that watching keeps them distracted, whereas others feel uncomfortable. It's a personal decision, and you can decide at the last moment.

Part One of the Exam

The vaginal exam will be in three parts. It's good for you to be aware of this so that you don't think it's over when it isn't. The first part consists of a general overview of the external parts of your vagina, including the vaginal lips, the clitoris, the urethra, and the glands that produce lubrication. The doctor will wear rubber gloves as he or she opens your vaginal lips to look around, checking to make sure that there are no signs of disease. A strong light will be pointed at your genitals to help the doctor see as clearly as possible. The doctor will look for any inflammation, lesions, swelling, or warts and will check the appearance of your lubrication. If you're using the mirror, the doctor will point out to you the various parts. Hopefully, the doctor will say that everything looks great. If you don't shave your pubic hair, the doctor will also look through it to check for lice or nits.

If you're a virgin, you may wonder why the doctor has to look for signs of sexually transmitted diseases. The problem with the word *virgin* is that these days it has several meanings. Is someone who has had oral sex a virgin? Is a woman who had sex only with another woman still a virgin? If someone inserted a finger into your vagina, are you still a virgin? Technically yes, because there has been no risk of pregnancy, but oral sex, as well as being masturbated by someone else or having a finger inserted into the vagina, can lead to the transmission of disease. Even if the doctor has asked a patient for a detailed sexual history, which may or may not always be truthful, the safer approach is for the doctor to do a thorough examination.

The doctor will be not only looking but also palpating, that is, touching and squeezing various body parts between his or her fingers. The doctor is looking for swelling of any kind, which could indicate a cyst below the surface of the skin that would not be visible. More of this palpating will happen during the third part of the exam.

If you've mentioned any problems, the doctor may use either a magnifying lens or a colposcope to take a closer look. Genital warts, for example, which are an STD, may exist in only a microscopic size so that neither you nor the doctor could detect them without using magnification. This is why it's important to mention any complaints you might have, such as occasional itching or burning, because without this information the doctor might assume that your vagina is entirely healthy, based only on the observations he or she can make with the naked eye.

Some women worry that they might become excited by the examination. For most women, this process isn't at all sexy, and there is no possibility of becoming excited. For some it is sexy, though, especially if they give in to having sexual fantasies (These sexual feelings can arise even if the doctor is female, which doesn't mean that you are a lesbian, but only that the situation of having your genitals exposed is what you find arousing). Most of the time, a woman's arousal isn't publicly announced, as happens with men, but that's not necessarily true when the gynecologist is examining you, because if you start to produce extra lubrication, your doctor will probably notice. That's why there's a chaperone in the room so that no one gives in to any temptation.

If you have any questions, feel free to ask them. What questions might you have? Here are some typical ones:

Is my vagina normal looking? Even if a woman is very familiar with her own vagina, she may not have seen many others, certainly not up front and personal. So you might want to know something about the appearance of your vagina. The vaginal lips have many different shapes, and you might think that yours are somehow odd. The doctor can assure you that you are perfectly normal in this respect.

Is my clitoris too big or too small? The clitoral hood is not the same on all women. Feel free to ask questions about your clitoris, in terms of both its appearance (in addition to differences in the hood, the size of the clitoris also varies greatly) and functioning.

Why do I have a vaginal discharge? This may be completely normal, but sometimes a vaginal discharge can be a sign of something wrong, such as an infection. If you think that you have too much discharge, especially if it's discolored or it smells, ask the doctor about it. If you feel that you are not lubricating sufficiently during sex, this would be the time to speak up, because the doctor is looking at the glands that produce lubrication.

Why am I spotting? Once in a while, women might discover some blood in their urine when they urinate or notice that the urine has a different color. Or they find that they are spotting, with small blood stains on their panties, even when they are not having their menstrual period. Oftentimes, it's not easy to know for sure where the blood is coming from. Is it from the vagina, the urine, or even the rectum? Although the cause is, more often than not, completely harmless, such spotting could also be a sign of a problem. If you haven't mentioned this before, now would be a good time, so that the doctor can take a closer look during part two of the exam. (See "From Dr. Amos's Office: Emily's Story," later in the chapter, for more about spotting.)

Part Two of the Exam

Part two of the exam requires that the doctor insert a device, called a speculum, into your vagina.

If you are a virgin, meaning that you've never had vaginal intercourse, there is a chance that your hymen is intact, although it's possible that the hymen is not complete anymore. The hymen is a fold of tissue that partly covers the entrance to the vagina. Women are usually born with most of their hymens covering their vaginas. Not having an intact hymen does not mean that you are not a virgin anymore because the hymen could break during exercises or when you insert a tampon. By the way, the word *hymen* comes from Greek mythology and means "the god of marriage."

If your hymen is still intact, let the doctor know before the exam; then the doctor will proceed very cautiously with this part of the exam. Inserting the speculum could tear your hymen, and even though you would still be a virgin, a state that requires intercourse in order to end, the doctor understands that you may, like many women, prefer that your hymen remain intact until you decide to have intercourse.

Some of you may say to yourselves, "But wait a minute, don't I need this part of the exam?" You might, but it also depends on the reason for the speculum examination. If you've never had sex, then it's less likely that you've caught a sexually transmitted disease. Because another important aspect of the speculum examination is to test for cervical cancer via a Pap test, which is caused, for the most part, by an STD, the HPV virus (more on that in chapter 5), you may not have an urgent need for a Pap test unless there are other reasons.

If you are at the gynecologist's because you have other symptoms that require the doctor to examine your cervix more closely, he or she will ask whether you will allow your hymen to be broken and part two of the exam performed. (Inserting the speculum gently may not always tear the hymen, but because there are no guarantees, you'll have to assume the risk.) For the gynecologist to peer inside your vagina, all the way to the back where the cervix is located, he or she will have to spread your vagina apart a bit. This is done through the use of a speculum, a device that is placed inside your vagina (it looks a little like a duck's bill and is made of metal or plastic). When the speculum is slowly opened, it gently widens your vaginal opening so that the doctor can see inside your vagina, not only the entrance. You will feel this, it may be a bit uncomfortable, but it shouldn't cause you any actual pain. If it does, don't be stoic; speak up. Pain that is not supposed to occur could be a sign of something else that the doctor will want to investigate.

One cause of discomfort from the placement of the speculum could be that you are subconsciously constricting your vaginal muscles. This can be a problem when you have sex, causing painful intercourse, called dyspareunia, a subject I'll cover in chapter 5. If such a tightening occurs during the course of your exam, your doctor will talk to you about it. Yet this is not something you should expect to happen.

One complaint that women used to have was that the speculum was cold. Today doctors have gotten the message, and the speculum will usually have been slightly warmed. If for some reason it's cold, let your doctor know. It will also be well lubricated so that it slides in easily.

The next thing the gynecologist will do once your vagina has been opened up is take a Pap smear. "Pap" is an abbreviation for "Papanicolaou," and the test is named after Georgios Papanicolaou, the physician who researched vaginal cytology in the middle of the last century at New York's Cornell Medical School (incidentally, the same one where Dr. Amos works).

To do the Pap test, your doctor will insert a stick or a brush into your vagina, and scrape off a few cells from your cervix (this should be a painless procedure, although some women do complain of a little pain). The cells will be placed on a slide or into a solution and sent to a lab for analysis. The lab will be able to tell whether you have any abnormal cells, which could be precancerous or might actually mean you have cancer.

You should get the results of your Pap test in about one to three weeks, and I recommend that you always find out what the results are. If the result is anything but normal, you'll have to repeat the Pap test more often, get treated, or have other tests done. (I'll go into this in more detail in chapter 5.)

How often you should have a Pap test depends on several factors, and guidelines vary from country to country. In the past, the ACOG guidelines recommended a Pap test when you turned twenty-one or when you started having sex, and then every year thereafter. If you were older than thirty and in a monogamous relationship and you had had normal Pap tests for three years in a row, screening was not necessary every single year. The younger you started having sex, however, and the more partners you have had, the more important it is to go for a regular Pap test.

In November 2009, the recommendations for having a Pap test were changed by the ACOG. Here are the most recent guidelines:

- At age twenty-one, cervical cancer screening should begin (regardless of sexual history).
- Screening before age twenty-one should be avoided because women younger than twenty-one have a very low risk of cancer.
- Between the ages of twenty-one years and twenty-nine years, cervical cytology screening is recommended every two years.
- At age thirty, if a woman has no history of cervical cancer and has had three normal Pap tests in a row, she can be screened every three years, rather than every two to three years.
- Women who have undergone total hysterectomies no longer need a Pap test.
- Women ages sixty-five and older can discontinue cervical cancer screening if they have had three consecutive negative Pap tests and no abnormal tests in the previous ten years.

Right after the Pap test, the doctor may also do additional tests, which include testing for sexually transmitted diseases such as chlamydia and gonorrhea. In these tests, a special swab is dipped into the cervix and the vagina. The swab is then placed in a container and sent to the laboratory.

From Dr. Amos's Office: Christina's Story

A patient came to see me for her first visit and told me that she previously had an abnormal Pap smear but couldn't remember what it was. She was very concerned that she was at risk of developing cancer. I repeated her Pap test, and it was normal, but I asked her to get me a copy of her previous results. When I received the copy, the results showed that her prior Pap test had a condition named ASC-US or atypical squamous cells of undetermined significance. This helped me do another test for HPV, or human papilloma virus, which was negative. Fortunately, her being negative for HPV proved that there was no increased risk. This example shows how important it is to know the exact name of the diagnosis so that your doctor can determine its significance.

If you have an abnormal discharge, the doctor may also put a sample of the discharge on a glass slide and examine it under a microscope.

Part Three of the Exam

After having done the Pap test and the STD tests, the doctor will do a "bimanual" exam of your vagina and your internal organs. First, the doctor will put one or two fingers inside your vagina and then place his or her other hand on your abdomen. This will allow your doctor to feel if there is anything unusual in between. The doctor may not be able to see inside you, but by feeling, or palpating, the doctor can sometimes detect whether anything unusual is taking place, such as an abnormal size of the uterus or ovarian changes, such as cysts, and so forth.

During the bimanual examination, the doctor will also gently push your urethra up against your pelvic bone. This shouldn't cause any pain, but if you do feel pain, let your doctor know. The doctor is not trying to hurt you, and such pain is probably an indication of an infection.

From Dr. Amos's Office: The Transvaginal Ultrasound Exam

There is a good chance that in the near future, the bimanual examination will be replaced by a routine transvaginal ultrasound exam. Some doctors advocate doing a routine transvaginal ultrasound examination instead of a palpation of the uterus and the ovaries at the time of the yearly well-woman's examination. They argue that the bimanual examination is often difficult to interpret and does not reveal enough information about the pelvic organs, especially when the patient is obese. They feel that the sonogram provides much more information about the appearance and size of the uterus and the ovaries than the bimanual palpation examination does. The sonogram can act as an "eye" to look at the uterus, the ovaries, and other pelvic organs to improve detection of any possible problems. To perform a transvaginal sonogram, your gynecologist must be trained in this procedure and must have the right equipment available.

Next, the doctor will push up against your bladder, so make sure to urinate and empty your bladder before the examination. The doctor's palpation should cause you to feel the urge to urinate. Again, if you feel any pain, it could indicate a urinary tract infection, so it's important that the doctor conduct this test.

The next possible test involves inserting one finger in your vagina and one in your rectum. This allows your doctor to feel for other potential problems. Not every doctor will conduct this test in women under fifty, but many will. By this point, you'll have been sufficiently prodded that you won't care, but again, the point of doing this is to investigate whether any medical problems are present that your doctor could not detect any other way.

At the end of this exam, your doctor will know a lot more about your physical state, including whether you're a virgin, whether you might have any STDs, and whether you are or have ever been pregnant.

From Dr. Amos's Office: Emily's Story

A woman came to see me and reported that she was spotting, that is, she had found spots of blood in her panties or in her urine in between her monthly periods. After inserting the speculum into her vagina so that I could see her cervix, I noticed a small growth in her cervical canal, and when I touched it, it bled. I was able to biopsy a small part of this growth and remove it. The growth turned out to be a cervical polyp, and after its removal, the spotting ceased. I sent the polyp to be tested, and it was benign, meaning "not cancerous." Most of these polyps are noncancerous, and in this case, no trace of cancer was found. I also ordered a sonogram of her uterus, to make sure there was no other cause for the spotting. Yet that was merely a precaution because I was fairly certain that the polyp was the only reason for the bleeding.

The purpose of this woman's visit had been to find the source of the spotting and to stop the bleeding. She was young and hadn't yet had children, and because such polyps can interfere with getting pregnant, in this case it was good that the polyp had caused the spotting. This allowed me to remove it and thus ensure that when she wanted to have a child, she wouldn't face this particular barrier. I told her that when she was ready to get pregnant to come to me for an exam so that I could make sure she hadn't developed any new polyps, because the presence of one could indicate that she had a tendency to produce them.

A Full Exam

Although you may be anxious about the pelvic exam and might want it to begin and end as quickly as possible, your gynecologist will usually examine more than your vagina and will probably begin elsewhere. The exact order of your overall exam depends on how the gynecologist likes to operate, so there will be some variations with each doctor. A gynecologist is concerned with your overall health, not only with the state of your genitals, so the doctor will often listen to your heart and lungs with a stethoscope and examine your nose and ears. Your doctor will palpate your

---

From Dr. Amos's Office: Kim's Story

A forty-one-year-old patient of mine who had three children came to see me with complaints of feeling pressure in the lower part of her abdomen, together with increased vaginal bleeding. At her exam a year earlier, I'd noted the presence of fibroids in her uterus. At that time, they were about the size of a twelve-week-old pregnant uterus. Now that she could actually feel them, I knew they must have grown. By performing a manual exam, with two fingers inside her vagina and pushing down with my other hand on her abdomen, I was able to feel the fibroids. I noted that they were now about the size of a twenty-two- to twenty-four-week pregnant uterus. A transvaginal ultrasound confirmed the presence of several large-size fibroids of the uterus, which are benign growths. I discussed my findings with her and told her that in view of the increase in uterine size, as well as her physical complaints, it was my recommendation that they really should come out. As is the case for most of my unusual findings, I sent her to get a second opinion from another doctor, who confirmed that surgery was needed. She was then scheduled for a hysterectomy, the removal of her uterus. Her ovaries would not be removed so that her hormone levels would remain stable, but she would not be able to have any more children.

---

abdomen; examine your extremities, which can indicate other problems; and perform other examinations before beginning the pelvic exam.

Your Skin

Your doctor may also examine your skin, because malignant skin cancer such as melanoma is among the most frequent cancers for women between twenty-five and thirty-five years of age. Women with light skin, those with freckles and whose skin burns easily from the sun, those who live in the Sun Belt states, and those with a personal or family history of skin cancers are at a higher risk. You yourself can't examine many parts of your skin, such as your back, so your visit to the gynecologist is a great opportunity to get your skin checked out. It usually takes only a couple of minutes for the doctor to examine you for suspicious skin lesions, and you may want to remind your gynecologist to do this checkup if he or she hasn't. You will usually be referred to a dermatologist if your gynecologist finds something that needs a further examination.

Breast Examination

With breast cancer so prevalent, a close examination of your breasts will definitely be a part of any visit to the gynecologist. Your doctor will first take a look at your breasts with your arms at your sides and elevated. The next step is usually a palpation of both of your breasts, to look for any unusual lumps or breast changes. Although a lump may not indicate anything serious, if your doctor finds one, you will most likely be sent for a mammogram. Your doctor will encourage you to go for regular mammograms, no matter what. Sometimes when a mass is found, the gynecologist will refer you to a surgeon to biopsy the mass. If you've experienced any discharges from your breasts, especially if the discharge is bloody, or you regularly feel any pain, be sure to mention these conditions to your doctor.

If you are not familiar with how to do a breast self-examination, your doctor will show you what to do. Although this lesson is important, it's even more crucial that you actually make use of what you learn and examine your breasts once a month. It doesn't take long, and if you do it often enough, you'll have a good sense of how they feel so that if an abnormality should develop, you'll be able to tell right away.

Talking to Your Doctor

When the doctor asks you questions, obviously you will need to answer those questions. Yet you may have other questions of your own, either those you've thought of before the exam or some that occurred to you during the exam. How you ask your questions will depend somewhat on your personality and on how the doctor works best.

Many doctors report that patients suddenly pose a question while standing with one hand on the doorknob, as they're about to leave. Why do they wait so long? Perhaps they needed time to compose themselves to ask the question, especially if it's a bit embarrassing. Or maybe, with everything else that was going on, they forgot. Whatever the reason, the last second is not the best time to ask an important question. (If it's only something like, "When will I get the results of my test?" that's another story.)

If you thought of questions before you arrived at the doctor's office, you should definitely write them down. This has several advantages. The first is, you won't forget them (unless you leave the piece of paper you wrote them on at home!). Also, reading a question may be easier than thinking of what to say on the spur of the moment. Or, you could hand the doctor your list of questions. The doctor might decide to answer you then and there or, if time is short, may answer later by phone, mail, fax, or e-mail.

If you prepare this list of questions ahead of time, it might be a good idea to ask the doctor whether you could send them before you arrive for your exam. Your list of questions will be in your chart, and the doctor will answer them at the most opportune moment. Sending your questions ahead of time may be beneficial because one or more questions might affect the exam itself, for example, if the doctor has to look for the cause of a pain you've experienced.

Another big advantage of writing down your questions is that it can reduce your embarrassment. If any of your questions are sexual in nature, you might find it easier to express them in written form. Then, if the nurse is in the room, the doctor can ask her to leave on seeing the nature of your questions.

While it's always been a good idea to write down your questions, in this age of e-mail there might be other advantages. Dr. Amos prefers to answer his patients' questions via e-mail: "During the day, I am so busy that sometimes I can't devote the necessary time to answering all of the questions a patient might have. But if a patient e-mails me a question, I can answer it later in the day or at night and also include extra information, such as a link to a trustworthy website that could supply diagrams."

Of course, if you have an embarrassing question, it's possible that the doctor might be almost as embarrassed to answer the question in person as you are to ask it. Yet an e-mailed question is often much easier to answer, plus you then have it in writing so that you can refer back to it, whereas if the doctor gives you information orally, you might forget some or all of the details by the time you get home.

These days, doctors face more and more questions based on what patients have read on the Internet. This can be a good thing, as it can educate patients about issues they know little about. Yet because there are few systems to review what goes on the Internet, this can also lead to problems. Patients may get the wrong information or not fully understand what they read. In addition, all doctors bring to their practice the personal knowledge they've

From Dr. Amos's Office: Lauren's Story

I received a frantic phone call from a patient who then sent me an e-mail with a photo of her external genitalia attached. She saw something there and thought she had found a similar picture on the Internet showing cancer of the vagina. I gave her an appointment for the next day, and an examination revealed that everything was normal. What the patient saw turned out to be the external orifice of her urethra, the opening from which her urine is ejected during urination. This example shows that the Internet can be helpful but also very confusing. Instead of getting frightened by pictures you find on the Internet, you will often receive the best information from a visit to the doctor and an exam.

accumulated. Most of the time their experience will agree with the medical literature, but sometimes it doesn't. Believe it or not, sometimes the medical literature isn't in agreement, either. So if you trust your doctor, it's best to listen to what he or she has to say. That doesn't mean you shouldn't ask about something you read on the web. You just have to make sure the website is reputable. Don't automatically assume that the information is correct. Ask your question in such a way that the doctor is sure to understand that you're not second-guessing him or her but are merely curious. If you are too accusatory, the doctor will get defensive, and then nobody benefits.

I hope that after reading this chapter, you will be less afraid to undergo a gynecological exam and will also feel that you've gained valuable knowledge about yourself.

5

What Can Go Wrong

In this chapter, you'll probably learn more than you want to know about sexually transmitted diseases. Today, the age group that you might think needs this information the least—senior citizens—has the fastest-rising rate of STDs. Don't assume that you already know everything you need to. Please read this chapter carefully.

We all encounter health problems that need medical attention from time to time. Gynecologists treat a wide range of women's conditions, from pregnancy issues and deliveries to the very common vaginal infections to much more complicated problems that may require more extensive treatments, including surgery.

This is one more reason that I strongly urge you to go for preventative care. Not only do regular checkups prevent minor problems that you might not even know you have from turning into major ones, but these checkups also permit you to "interview" doctors so that you can find one you feel comfortable with and who has your full confidence. If you wait until you develop a medical condition before you look for a doctor, your treatment may be delayed until you find the right doctor or you might have to be treated by someone who doesn't fulfill your needs.

Sexually Transmitted Diseases

You will never hear me use the phrase "safe sex." Instead, I say "safer sex," because there really is no such thing as safe sex. Why is it important not to say "safe sex"? Because when you hear that phrase over and over again, you fall into the delusion that it exists. Instead, you have to keep telling yourself that because it's impossible to know whether the person you are with is "safe," it's better to take every precaution. And because even that won't guarantee that you remain safe, it's vital that you have sex only with someone you really care for, so that if you do catch something, at least you might be able to save the relationship. But if you contract a disease from having sex with a person you don't love, you'll really regret it for the rest of your life.

Sexually transmitted diseases (STDs) are infections transmitted through sex or other intimate contact. You can usually decrease your chances of becoming infected with a sexually transmitted disease by taking precautions, which include not engaging in risky sex and using protection, such as condoms. Let's begin with the ideal situation for keeping you free from STDs, while you are still sexually active. If you have never had sex with anyone else and your partner never had sex with anyone else, then when the two of you have sex, there will be no chance of your transmitting an STD to each other. That makes sense, right? So what are the pitfalls? Let's start with that word *sex.*

These days, someone could be a virgin and still have had sex with lots of different people. The person may never have had intercourse, but even kissing (or touching) can pass along certain sexually transmitted diseases. Or, they could have engaged in oral sex, anal sex, and mutual masturbation, and any one of those acts could potentially spread a disease (I'm not talking about self-masturbation, even if someone else is watching; I mean only if one person is stimulating the other with physical contact).

If you have a partner who says he or she has never had sex with anyone else, the first thing you have to ascertain is what that means. If this person has had intimate physical contact with another person, then you have to assume that this person could infect you with an STD.

Can you get an STD from kissing? For a long time, the answer to that question would have been no. But today, because so many more people are engaging in oral sex, the answer is yes. Herpes is just one example. There are two types of herpes viruses, herpes type 1 (HSV-1) and type 2 (HSV-2). HSV-1 is more common in infections of the mouth and the lips but can also infect the genitals, and HSV-2 more often infects the genitals but can infect the mouth. Doctors are seeing many more cases of genital herpes (HSV-2) appearing as "cold sores," which used to be the exclusive domain of HSV-1. And vice versa, they're finding HSV-1 on people's genitals. So if your partner has genital herpes in and around his mouth, he could potentially infect you with genital herpes while kissing.

Another problem when assessing the risk of getting an STD is that you can't be sure whether a potential partner is telling the truth. Someone could appear to be the most honest person in the world and yet be lying. In matters of sex, people often do lie because they might be ashamed of the behavior that led them to get an STD, such as a one-night stand after getting drunk or paying a prostitute. In other cases, a person might be infected with an STD and not know it. Many STDs can be caught without showing any visible signs. Yet the person who catches one of these diseases without knowing it can still pass it on, and the next person who gets it, potentially you, might get a full-blown case.

The Limits of Testing

Let's suppose you are a heterosexual woman, and you meet somebody new. You tell him that you won't have sex with him unless he gets tested for STDs. He says he got tested and shows you the results, which are negative. You then have sex with him. Are you safe? You could be but certainly not 100 percent safe. There are two reasons for this. The first has to do with the testing process. Some STDs, including the most dangerous one, HIV, don't always show up in test results until several months after the infection first started. So, if someone was infected by the HIV virus a month ago, it won't necessarily show up in the tests. If you then start having sex with this person, you could get infected. In fact, you are more likely to become infected with HIV if you have sex shortly after your partner first became infected. Also, some tests are more precise than others. Certain tests catch every instance of the infection (if possible, given the previous caveat), and others don't, yet many doctors are not aware of the differences. This is another reason why someone who's been tested might not be disease-free. Finally, just because someone took a test yesterday doesn't mean that he might not have sex with someone else tomorrow and catch a disease that he'll pass on to you. That's true even if you are in a monogamous relationship and even if you're married. Married people do cheat. Not every married person cheats, but enough do that the risks are always present.

The Efficiency of Condoms

Condoms offer you a great deal of protection against catching many STDs, but they are far from 100 percent effective for several reasons. First of all, a condom can break or fall off. If that happens, you're no longer protected. Also, some people don't know how to use them correctly, or they don't use condoms every single time. If in the heat of the moment they don't have a condom, they might risk having sex anyway. Finally, condoms protect only your genitals. As you'll see in the section on herpes, people who are infected with herpes can be shedding viruses from various parts of their anatomy, including the thighs and the buttocks. Certainly, condom use won't protect you against viruses spread by those body parts. So although you should always use condoms unless you are as sure as possible that it's safe not to, you can't rely on condoms to fully protect you.

Take Precautions

The urge to have sex is so strong that despite the risks, people are still having sex in situations that are less than ideal, in terms of protecting themselves from getting an STD. That's why so many tens of millions of people are infected with one STD or another. Now, you might be tempted to say to yourself, "Since I can't really protect myself, and I don't want to be celibate, why bother even trying to protect myself?" I have to give you the facts, but please don't stop taking whatever actions you can to protect yourself from STDs. No one can say exactly how effective your efforts will be, but just be as careful as possible. You may not be able to make having sex 100 percent safe, but if you can get it to 90 percent, that's certainly worth attempting.

The one attitude I want you to avoid at all costs, however, is thinking that it doesn't matter if you catch an STD because medicine can always cure you. Nothing is further from the truth. In some cases, medicine can cure you; in other cases, it can cure you, but the damage to your body has already been done. When it comes to the most serious of STDs, HIV/AIDS, there is no permanent cure. Although certain "cocktails" of drugs can help you survive longer, they do not eradicate the virus forever, they are quite costly, and they're not without side effects. Plus, you can still transmit the virus to others even though you are taking medication.

Finally, while the other STDs won't kill you, they can increase your chances of getting something worse. It's been shown that people who have sores from herpes infections have an increased chance of getting infected with other diseases, including HIV.

So although herpes itself won't kill you, it brings the added danger of making you more susceptible to getting HIV, which *can* kill you. That's true for many other STDs as well. For that reason alone, it's worth doing whatever you can to protect yourself against all STDs.

HIV and AIDS

Human immunodeficiency virus (HIV) is the virus that causes AIDS, which stands for acquired immunodeficiency syndrome. *Acquired* means that the disease develops from being exposed to a disease-causing agent (in this case, HIV), and *immunodeficiency* means that it is characterized by a weakening of the immune system. *Syndrome* is a group of symptoms that collectively indicates or characterizes a disease. AIDS, for example, includes the development of certain infections and/or cancers and a weakening of the person's immune system.

We know that herpes has been around since the days of the ancient Greek empire, and other STDs have been with humans for hundreds of years (and maybe longer, though they may not have been identified). Yet while the existence of these diseases was known, the danger was limited in scope. Then in the late 1970s and the early 1980s, AIDS was first found to be spreading among homosexual communities, then eventually among other communities. A few years later, it was discovered that AIDS was caused by the human immunodeficiency virus, and the nature of STDs was changed forever, from an annoyance to something deadly.

HIV attacks the body's immune system, leaving its victims prone to many different types of diseases. HIV itself doesn't kill, but the virus makes its victims very vulnerable to other diseases, which are potentially fatal. In fact, it was the number of cases of certain very rare cancers among the homosexual community that prompted scientists to look for an underlying cause.

HIV is transmitted during sexual activity, and that includes intercourse, anal sex, and oral sex. You can get infected with HIV (and many other STDs) any time you are in contact with infected secretions or fluids. Every time mucous membranes touch each other (such as during kissing or sex) or you touch membranes, secretions, or body fluids, there is a chance of getting an HIV infection. HIV cannot live for too long outside the body, so it is unlikely to be transferred through everyday contact, such as shaking hands or touching an object that has been touched by someone infected with HIV. Because HIV is transmitted in the bodily fluids, condom use can decrease but not always fully prevent the spread of HIV, and in fact, as condom use has spread due to the fear of contracting AIDS, the number of people infected has gone down. Yet since many people infected with HIV don't yet know that they have the disease, it is important for everyone who engages in risky sex, such as sex with multiple partners, to remain vigilant.

Women are more likely to become infected from men who are HIV positive than the other way around. Then there are babies who can become infected from their mothers. This infection can happen inside the uterus, at birth, or from breast-feeding.

The HIV virus can also be transferred intravenously, meaning with the use of a needle. Drug addicts who share needles are at great risk of getting HIV. In addition, HIV can be transmitted to an unborn child from a mother infected with the virus, as well as to a baby via breast-feeding.

It's wonderful that we can now keep people who've been infected with HIV alive for many more years, but there is a downside. Some young people who hear of this have begun to engage in risky sexual practices. They're too young to have experienced all of the deaths that AIDS caused, and they have this feeling that if they happen to get AIDS, these drugs will save them. But there are gaping holes in this argument. The first is that these drugs are very expensive. Yes, some insurance plans will cover them, but not every plan and not forever. Second, these drugs have side effects. You may escape the immediate death sentence of AIDS, but your quality of life will decrease considerably.

If you are infected with HIV, you must tell any potential sexual partners of your status, even if you are going to use a condom. If a condom were to break and this person were to be exposed to HIV without being told ahead of time, the consequences would be quite serious. You might even face legal ramifications. Yet more important, there is a moral imperative to tell someone that this risk exists, even if it is a person whom you may never see again (not that I advocate casual sex, but I know it happens, and the two people involved must communicate about any potential risks from STDs).

By the way, although I am telling you to use condoms to prevent transmitting diseases, it's important that you understand that only latex or other synthetic condoms protect against the transmission of disease. Lambskin condoms can protect against pregnancy, but they have pores that are large enough to permit viruses to get through.

If you are going to have sex with a new partner, and either of you has previously had sex with other people, then it is highly advisable for each of you to be tested for STDs, and HIV in particular. This is especially important because someone infected with HIV might not show any symptoms for quite a while. To be protected, however, you need to be aware of how these tests work. Of course, once someone is tested and has a negative result, if he or she subsequently has sex with another person, that test result is worthless. So, in addition to relying on testing to protect yourself, you should have sex only with someone you are in a close relationship with and whom you trust to remain monogamous.

Although testing is an important armor to protect yourself against getting HIV, the waiting period means that a lot of people who find themselves swept off their feet don't bother to wait to get tested and receive the results. It would be great if everyone used testing the optimal way, but it's also unrealistic to expect that people will do so. In addition, certain people lie and say they've tested negative for HIV and haven't had sex with anybody since then, when that isn't true. That's why it's vital that you use condoms if you have sex when you are not in a long-term relationship. If you do find yourself in such a situation and a relationship does form, then you can both get tested, and if you both test negative and are using another method of birth control, you can stop using condoms. But until you are as sure as you can be that you are safe from HIV, never have sex without using a condom.

Having said that, I am also aware that people engage in oral sex. A woman could be protected by making sure the penis is covered by a condom, but a man or a woman giving oral sex to another woman is unlikely to use a dental dam or at least not be able to use it without the risk of ingesting some fluid. It is less likely that you will contract HIV via oral sex, but it is certainly not impossible. At the very least, don't fool yourself into thinking that oral sex is safe, and to fully protect yourself, don't perform oral sex unless you are sure the other person is disease-free.

Chlamydia

With more than a million new cases reported to the Centers for Disease Control each year (and that's only counting those that are reported, because most people who have it don't even know they do), chlamydia is the most widespread STD in the country.

Chlamydia can be transferred from one individual to another via vaginal, anal, or oral sex. If both people in a couple have it, and only one is treated, the chances of having it retransmitted are high. Chlamydia can also be transmitted to a baby during childbirth if the mother is infected. Younger women who are sexually active are most likely to catch chlamydia because the cervix is still not fully developed, so it is more open to infection.

How do you know if you have chlamydia? Three-fourths of women don't know because they don't sense any symptoms, and only half of men do. Those who do experience symptoms will have a vaginal discharge and possibly a burning sensation when urinating. If the infection spreads to the woman's fallopian tubes, she may feel some lower back pain, abdominal pain, nausea, fever, and pain during intercourse, but even when it has spread, a woman may not feel anything.

As a result of being infected with chlamydia, 40 percent of women get pelvic inflammatory disease (PID). When this occurs, the woman will suffer permanent damage to her reproductive system, probably rendering her infertile. She may also experience chronic pelvic pain and may be subject to developing an ectopic pregnancy, a pregnancy where the egg implants itself outside the womb and which is very dangerous to the life of the mother. Finally, women with chlamydia are up to five times more susceptible to contracting HIV/AIDS.

It is very simple to cure chlamydia with a single antibiotic; however, if both partners aren't treated and the woman gets reinfected, the likelihood of damage to her reproductive system increases greatly.

Gonorrhea

The bacterium that causes gonorrhea spreads via sexual contact, through vaginal, anal, or oral sex. It thrives in moist places and in women will spread into the cervix, the uterus, the fallopian tubes, and the urethra. In men, it remains in the urethra, perfectly positioned to spread itself to a man's partner. An estimated seven hundred thousand new cases of gonorrhea are contracted each year in the United States.

As with chlamydia, most women who get gonorrhea don't have any symptoms or at least none that they might associate with the disease. (Not all men get symptoms, either, but men are more likely to have a white, yellow, or greenish discharge from their penis, as well as a burning sensation when they urinate.)

In women, just as with chlamydia, gonorrhea can lead to PID, so that a woman may become infertile if the disease reaches her fallopian tubes. It can also lead to an ectopic pregnancy, which can be life threatening. Gonorrhea can even spread to the blood or the joints, which is a dangerous condition.

Gonorrhea has been easily treated with several antibiotics, and because it is often accompanied by chlamydia, the two are usually treated together. Yet new strains that are resistant to antibiotics have cropped up, and they are spreading worldwide, including in the United States. Although the strains that do respond to antibiotics will be killed if you are treated, any damage that has been done to your reproductive system cannot be repaired, so it's important to get treatment as soon as possible.

If you discover that you have one of these STDs, whether the two I've already covered or any other, please be sure to tell every single person with whom you've had sex that he or she is at risk of having this disease, too, and needs to see a doctor to be tested. Because these diseases don't necessarily have symptoms, it is vitally important that people exposed to the bacterium are warned. Otherwise, the disease will continue to spread, potentially either rendering innocent women infertile, causing an ectopic pregnancy that could be deadly, or opening them up to the possibility of getting AIDS. Yes, this is an embarrassing conversation to have. Yes, some people may get angry with you. You might lose a friendship or two, but to remain silent and pretend nothing happened is just immoral.

If a pregnant woman has gonorrhea that is left untreated, it can be passed on to the baby as the baby goes through the birth canal and can cause blindness, joint infection, or a blood infection that could even be fatal.

Hepatitis B

Hepatitis in general is an inflammation of the liver. Infectious hepatitis (as compared to other types of liver inflammation) is caused by various types of viruses, such as hepatitis A, hepatitis B, and hepatitis C virus. Rarer forms include hepatitis D and E.

Hepatitis A is rarely sexually transmitted but is usually transmitted through ingesting contaminated food or water or sharing contaminated utensils. It normally clears up quickly and does not result in serious diseases.

Hepatitis B and C are two forms of the hepatitis virus that can be transmitted via sexual contact but also through contact with membranes, blood transfusions, and at birth from mother to baby.

Most people who get hepatitis B or C show no symptoms, although they can pass the virus on to others. If the signs of infection do occur, they can take up to six months and generally include flulike symptoms but may also produce jaundice, which makes your skin and the whites of your eyes turn yellow. If you get hepatitis B, you stand a 10 percent chance of developing a chronic liver infection that can lead to cirrhosis of the liver (which kills liver cells) and even liver cancer. Both hepatitis B and C can result in chronic carrier status, where the infected person can transmit it to someone else, and both B and C can also develop into chronic illnesses, destroying the liver over time and leading to liver cancer and death.

Condoms help prevent the spread of hepatitis B, which is very easily transmitted, and today many young people are vaccinated against the virus. There is no cure for hepatitis B. All that doctors can do is help relieve the symptoms.

All pregnant women get tested for the presence of the hepatitis B virus. If they carry the virus, they can transmit it to the baby, so the baby will get a shot of immunoglobulin and will be vaccinated at birth.

Immunization against the hepatitis B virus is available and very effective. It is recommended for anyone who has been exposed to the virus, such as health-care workers, and others who want to be protected. Babies are often immunized at birth.

Herpes

Herpes isn't only one disease but is more like a family. Among its relatives, for example, is chicken pox. What has changed about herpes is that instead of there being only one type of herpes that attacks the genitals, there are now two, because oral herpes has been diagnosed more and more often in the genital region, thanks to the growth in popularity of oral sex.

There are two herpes viruses, HSV-1 and HSV-2. What we call "genital herpes" was traditionally caused by the HSV-2 virus but can also occur with the HSV-1 virus. What we have long called a "cold sore" is often caused by the virus HSV-1 but sometimes also by HSV-2. In the past, HSV-1 was found exclusively above the waist and HSV-2 below the waist, and although that remains generally true, the number of exceptions is growing. So what might appear to be a case of genital herpes, that is, HSV-2, on your genitals could actually be HSV-1. The only reason this should matter to you is if you thought that engaging in oral sex, rather than genital sex, was "safe" with respect to the transmission of STDs, and the answer is, it's not.

The rise of herpes came about just before the appearance of AIDS, and a lot of evidence indicates that this is not a coincidence. Yet although herpes got a lot of media attention at one point, once AIDS came along, herpes dropped back into the pack of STDs. While it was the "hot" STD, however, people were very concerned about getting herpes because of the awful sores and pain associated with the disease. Now it's true that herpes can cause severe outbreaks of sores that are ugly and painful, but the fact is that most people who are infected with herpes don't even know it. They may have no outward signs whatsoever, or else they may get one tiny sore, and if it's located within a woman's vagina, she'll never realize it. Yet just because she never gets a major outbreak doesn't mean that she can't pass it on, and the next person may get just such a major outbreak. Because so many people who are sexually active don't know they are infected, it's estimated that forty-five million Americans older than twelve, one in four women (as compared to one in eight men), have been infected. One reason that herpes is so widespread is that it has a little trick up its sleeve that is not shared by other STDs. Most STDs can be transmitted only by genital-to-genital contact, because that's where the bacteria live.

From Dr. Amos's Office: Claudia's Story

A patient came to see me at eight weeks of her pregnancy. She informed me that her husband had a history of herpes, and she assumed she was also positive. A blood test showed that she tested negative for herpes antibodies and thus never had herpes, even though her husband was apparently positive. I explained to her the risks involved in becoming infected with herpes for the very first time in pregnancy, and we discussed precautions, which included using a condom at all times during intercourse to prevent an infection. This example shows that although condoms are most often used to prevent pregnancy, they can also be worn during pregnancy to prevent sexually transmitted diseases.

But the herpes virus can settle on other parts of the body, such as the thighs or the buttocks. When that happens, when a sexual partner of yours is shedding live viruses from some other part of his or her body than the genitals, condom use offers no protection. Someone could be shedding viruses and have absolutely no idea because there might not even be any visual sores.

A herpes attack can be painful. Herpes in a pregnant woman poses a potential risk for the child, because herpes could be transmitted during the baby's passage through the birth canal. If a woman giving birth is having an outbreak, a C-section will be performed. Herpes can also make you more likely to become infected with HIV. Yet perhaps the worst aspect of herpes is the psychological one.

HPV

Human papilloma virus (HPV) is the most common STD. At any one time, about twenty million people are infected, and it's thought that among sexually active people, 50 percent will become infected at some point in their lives. There are forty types of HPV, some of which cause genital warts and others that are thought to also cause cervical cancer, as well as other cancers. Those that cause genital warts are not necessarily the same as those that cause cancer. Most forms of HPV don't give any sign that the person has been infected, because even with most cases of genital warts, the warts are so small that they can be seen only inside the cells or with the aid of a microscope. Those that do not cause cancer are called low risk, and those that cause cancer are labeled high risk. In most cases, 90 percent, the body's immune system gets rid of HPV within two years without any treatment. The 10 percent of women who have high-risk HPV and their immune systems do not clear up the problem have a greater chance of developing cancer of the cervix or, much more rarely, other types of cancer, including cancer of the vagina, the vulva, or the anus.

In rare cases, a woman with HPV who gives birth can transmit the disease to her child as it passes through the birth canal, but the transmission risk is not high enough to recommend cesarean delivery in HPV-infected women.

Although condoms can help prevent the spread of HPV, they do not cover every part of the body where HPV may be, so they do not offer 100 percent protection. A vaccine against HPV has now been developed (this vaccine protects against most cervical cancers but not all of them). Given that HPV is so widespread and that eleven thousand women are diagnosed with cervical cancer every year (and another ten thousand with cancer of the vagina, the vulva, or the anus), having young women vaccinated against HPV is worth considering.

This vaccine is clearly a good thing, and it's wonderful that it has been invented. However, I'm not so sure that it's such a wise idea to have this vaccination process done as early as some people advocate, that is, at twelve years of age. Yes, there are some sexually active twelve-year-olds, and they deserve to be protected, but the vast majority of twelve-year-olds are not sexually active, and vaccinating girls at this age seems to send the wrong message.

Because HPV usually disappears within a year or two, most people are not urged to be tested for it. Yet because of the risk of getting cervical cancer, every woman should get a yearly Pap test to make sure that there are no signs of cancer on her cervix. (Whether those who practice anal sex should get a yearly Pap test on their anus is still being debated.)

While the body's immune system will get rid of the HPV infection, for people who do get visible genital warts and want them removed, both over-the-counter and other medicines can be applied.

Vaginal Infections

The most common problem that women develop is a vaginal infection. Your vagina is home to many different organisms. A few of them belong there, but many may not. Although the thought may bother you, this is the normal state of affairs, and there's nothing you should do about it. (That includes douching, which we do not recommend.) A few bacteria in your vagina are considered "good" (such as the so-called lactobacilli), because they are beneficial to the vagina's health. It is these lactobacilli, the good bacteria, that keep in check any other bacteria that might cause you harm. Yet sometimes this positive balance is thrown off. One of the most common causes of this type of imbalance is using antibiotics. If you're given antibiotics to treat a certain medical condition (such as a urinary tract infection or acne, for example), the antibiotics will also kill off many of the good bacteria in your vagina. This gives the other bacteria a chance to multiply, and you could then wind up with a vaginal infection.

If your vagina is itchy or painful, and the normal vaginal discharge has changed in some way, which includes an unusual odor, then you probably have vaginitis, or a vaginal infection. The majority of vaginitis cases stem from several different causes, such as yeast infections, bacterial vaginosis, trichomoniasis, and some sexually transmitted diseases, such as chlamydia and gonorrhea. Occasionally, vaginitis is sexually transmitted; other times it's not.

Some women repeatedly get a certain type of vaginitis, and if your doctor has diagnosed it before, then he or she may be willing to give you a prescription over the phone. Or if you suspect that you have an allergy, rather than an infection, you may be able to treat yourself by removing the allergen. If it's an infection, though, and you don't know what it is, I recommend that you don't guess and instead see your doctor.

What you wear may also be a factor in getting such irritations or infections. If you wear panties and/or pantyhose that don't breathe, you can create conditions that can lead to vaginal infections. It's best to wear cotton or at least have underwear that has cotton built into the crotch area. Also make sure to change your underwear daily, and if it's very hot and humid, don't wear pantyhose for too long a period of time, if possible. Or, when you are at home, don't wear tight underpants at all and let your vagina breathe!

I don't recommend that you use a vaginal douche. The companies that make vaginal douches try to convince women that this should be part of their daily routine, like brushing their teeth, but the truth is that these products can make things worse, not better. Douching changes the pH of your vagina, lowering the acidity, which can make you more prone to getting infections. If you actually have an infection, you should absolutely not douche, because the douche could push the germs deeper into your body, up into your uterus or fallopian tubes, where more serious problems could develop. You also don't want to douche right before going to the doctor, because that would change the appearance of what the doctor was trying to examine.

Yeast Infections

The organism responsible for a yeast infection is not a bacterium but a fungus called candida, and one of them, *Candida albicans*, is the most common one affecting the vagina. The more technical term for yeast vaginitis would be *candidiasis*. Candida can infect not only the vagina and the genitalia but also the mouth, the esophagus, the skin, and the intestinal tract.

If you have a vaginal or genital yeast infection, your vagina and your vulva (the area just outside your vagina) will probably be red and itchy. Your vaginal discharge, which is usually thick and white, will look more like cottage cheese, although it will probably have no smell. If the symptoms are only external, it's called vulvitis, though it's common to have both together, a condition that is then called vulvovaginitis.

Before treatment, it's important to see a gynecologist because you can't be sure what type of infection you may have without a medical diagnosis. The correct diagnosis will usually require a speculum examination, a microscopy examination, and a culture. The treatment for a yeast infection is a prescription cream that is applied either manually or via a suppository. You can also take pills, as well as some over-the-counter products. By the way, treating the infection may not end the itching and the swelling, so you may also need a topical ointment to handle those symptoms.

From Dr. Amos's Office: Treating Yeast Infections

If you get a yeast infection most of the times that you use an antibiotic, make sure to let your doctor know this (and that means any doctor, not only your gynecologist). Then apply an antiyeast infection cream to your vagina during the time you take the antibiotics. You may also discuss with your doctor whether you should use probiotics while taking antibiotics, to decrease the risk of candidiasis. One potential source of any vaginal infection could be your own fecal matter. Women should always wipe themselves from front to back to prevent any germs from the anus from coming into contact with the vagina, where they could cause an infection.

Yeast infections are thought to have little to do with sex, so women who are not sexually active can get yeast infections. Yet some women report that they get a yeast infection after having sex, and in those cases, it's probably wise to have the man treated as well.

Bacterial Vaginosis

If you feel itchy inside and around the vaginal entrance, and you have a thin, fishy smelling discharge, then you may have a vaginal infection called bacterial vaginosis, or BV. The main difference you'll notice between this type of infection and a yeast infection has to do with the accompanying vaginal discharge, which will be thin and milky and will probably have a "fishy" odor. If the symptoms are mild, and they often are, you could have this type of infection and not know it until you undergo a pelvic exam. Again, an examination by your gynecologist is necessary to make the right diagnosis.

The antibiotic prescribed for bacterial vaginitis may kill off the "bad" bacteria, while not harming the "good." It is available only by prescription.

Bacterial vaginosis sometimes goes away by itself, and many women don't seek treatment but just wait it out. If you're willing to put up with the discomfort, that's your decision; however, if you're pregnant and you get a vaginal infection such as BV, don't ignore it, because having an infection can increase certain risks, such as premature labor and delivery. Tell your doctor and begin taking antibiotics to ensure the health of your baby.

Trichomoniasis

Trichomoniasis, more commonly referred to simply as trich, is a sexually transmitted disease. Instead of bacteria being spread, the culprit is a protozoan, a single-cell parasite. Both men and women can get trich, but very often men don't have any symptoms, although they might feel some burning when they urinate, whereas women will more commonly have itchiness and sores, similar to other vaginal infections. There will also likely be a smell from the discharge, which is thin and greenish yellow and sometimes frothy.

Several antibiotics can be used to treat trich, and the outcome is almost always successful. You should avoid intercourse until all signs of the disease have disappeared. Of course, you should consider using condoms to avoid getting trich or any other STD.

Can you have sex with your partner if you have a vaginal infection? The answer to this question depends on two factors: what type of infection you have and how severe it is. If it's very severe, you may not even feel like having sex. If sex is uncomfortable because of the soreness of your vagina, then you certainly should refrain from having sex. If the infection is sexually transmitted, then your partner can contract it when you have sex, or if you get it treated and your partner doesn't, then you will likely get reinfected from having sex.

So, both partners must get treated at the same time if one partner has a treatable sexually transmitted disease. If only one partner gets treated, then she or he will get infected again by making love with the untreated partner.

If you have an STD, you should not have unprotected intercourse until both you and your partner are treated and are free of the disease to avoid reinfecting each other.

One exception is human papilloma virus, or HPV. If you have been diagnosed with HPV, there is no clear treatment that can eliminate the HPV, so you and your doctor should discuss how to deal with sexual issues.

Another exception is HIV. A person who is infected with HIV can infect another person during sexual intercourse. Women are more likely to become infected by men than the other way around. Because there is no final treatment for HIV, people with HIV can infect their sexual partners independent of whether they take medications.

So many couples think that "sex" consists only of intercourse, and prohibiting them from having intercourse can seem almost painful, adding to the misery of having a vaginal infection. Yet if one partner has a physical problem that prevents intercourse, it doesn't mean that each partner can't be sexually satisfied in other ways. Eventually, a vaginal infection will pass, but until that time, make sure that you don't become sexually frustrated simply because you can't have intercourse.

Urinary Tract Infections

Each year millions of women in the United States get urinary tract infections, or UTIs. A UTI occurs when bacteria get into the urethra and travel up into the bladder. There are several reasons why women are a lot more prone than men to getting UTIs. Being located just inside the vagina, the urethra comes into contact with outside microbes that are placed there during intercourse, and since a woman's urethra is much shorter than a man's, these germs can easily travel up into the bladder. Because the urethra may become irritated during intercourse, either from the friction or from the use of products such as condoms and spermicides, that irritation also increases the risk of infection. Pregnant women tend to get more UTIs because hormonal changes may relax the muscles of the urinary tract so that urine remains in the bladder, and postmenopausal women are at risk because the tissue in their urinary tract thins out due to the reduction of estrogen.

A UTI can sometimes have no symptoms, and then it's called asymptomatic UTI. You know you have asymptomatic UTI when you get a stinging or burning sensation while you urinate. You'll probably have the urge to "go" more often as well, even if there's little or no urine left in your bladder.

Although a UTI may get better on its own, if you continue to feel the symptoms after several days, call your doctor, and you'll be given antibiotics that will take care of it. Always make sure that you complete the full course of antibiotics. Stopping just because you don't feel any more symptoms is likely to lead to a reinfection soon afterward.

> **From Dr. Amos's Office: Preventing UTIs**
>
> Does cranberry juice work as a prevention for UTIs? Drinking cranberry juice makes your urine more acidic and is also thought to make it more difficult for bacteria to adhere to the bladder wall. Drinking cranberry juice is unlikely to treat a UTI, but some studies show that people who drink it regularly may decrease the incidence of UTIs.

Polycystic Ovarian Syndrome

Most women ovulate around a similar day of their cycles, so what it really boils down to is that whatever ovulation pattern you develop will then become your personal normal length. Women with very irregular cycle lengths, very long or very short cycles or no period at all, likely have a problem with their ovulation. They ovulate either irregularly or not at all, which can make it difficult for them to become pregnant.

The number-one cause of ovulation problems and irregular periods is a medical condition called polycystic ovarian syndrome, or PCOS. Your doctor can perform tests to find out if PCOS is the reason for your irregular cycles.

Significant weight gain or loss can trigger PCOS. If you are overweight, exercising and losing weight can often help you regulate your ovulation and your cycles. Stress can also affect your ovulation and menstrual cycles. When you're stressed out, your body produces excess cortisol, which affects your sex hormones, estrogen and progesterone, and, consequently, that can make your monthly

> **From Dr. Amos's Office: Reducing Stress**
>
> You might be tempted to reduce stress by smoking or drinking alcohol, but although you may perceive these to be stress reducers, your body takes the opposite view, which causes it to release even more cortisol and makes your medical condition worse.

cycle become irregular. Some women find that traveling across time zones also has this effect on them.

Fibroids

Fibroids or leiomyoma are growths of muscle tissue inside or on top of the uterus. They are benign and can vary in size from as small as an apple seed all the way up to as large as a grapefruit, and they can get even larger. They can grow singly or in clumps, and they may grow simultaneously in different areas of your uterus.

The medical community calls them "tumors," but a fibroid is not cancerous. If you have a mass growing in your uterus, and the doctor says you have fibroids, then you don't have cancer. But when a doctor discovers that something is growing, and before he or she knows for sure what it is, you will, of course, be quite nervous. Fibroids are very common; 25 percent of all women develop one or more fibroids by the time they're fifty, so the odds are in your favor that any growth is a fibroid and not cancer.

Most women who develop fibroids have no idea that they're present. Yet fibroids can cause some women a number of symptoms, including excessive menstrual bleeding, bleeding between periods, pelvic pain, back pain, and abdominal discomfort. Pressure on the bladder from large fibroids can cause a frequent urge to urinate, while pressure on the rectum can result in constipation. Women who are trying to become pregnant can encounter difficulties because of fibroids.

The tendency to develop fibroids is genetic, and African American women are three to nine times more likely to get fibroids than Caucasian women are. If you've never had children and you had an early menarche (first period), at age ten or younger, these factors can often lead to your developing fibroids.

Once you report symptoms to your doctor that would indicate the possibility of fibroids, your doctor has an assortment of different ways to check for them, starting with a pelvic exam and proceeding to an ultrasound, taking a tissue sample, doing a hysteroscopy (sending a small camera up through the cervix), and finally performing a laparoscopy.

Just because you have fibroids doesn't mean that they have to be treated. If you have few or no symptoms and are not planning to become pregnant, your doctor will likely recommend not doing anything. If you are troubled by excess bleeding, then your doctor might suggest putting you on birth control pills, which might increase the size of the fibroids but decrease any bleeding. Certain drugs will also lessen your production of estrogen, but although these drugs can reduce the size of a fibroid while you're on them, the side effects are similar to undergoing menopause, and if you're not prepared for that and decide to go off the drugs, the fibroids will recommence growing. It may be possible to remove the fibroids via a hysteroscopy and removal of the cervix, or a myomectomy. In either of these procedures, the uterus is left intact and the possibility of having children remains. If the fibroids are too big, however, the most likely surgical solution is a hysterectomy, during which the uterus will be removed, and you can no longer have children. Of the six hundred thousand hysterectomies performed in the United States yearly, two-thirds are done to remove fibroids.

Endometriosis

The inside lining of the uterus, the part that sheds monthly, causing your menstrual bleeding, is called the endometrium. Every month, once a woman begins having periods, her hormones trigger growth of the cells of the endometrium as it gets ready to host a fertilized egg. If no egg is implanted, these cells shed through the cervix and the vagina.

Endometriosis happens when the inside lining of the uterus implants elsewhere, such as the outside of the uterus, the fallopian tubes, the ovaries, or other areas. Every month they grow in size and can cause you quite a bit of problems and pain. The pain from endometriosis can be severe enough to be debilitating, and while this pain will probably be located in the pelvic area, which is the part of the body most likely to have such cells, the pain could stem from almost any part of the body where the cells happen to wind up.

Women who have never had children are most at risk, and a woman who has endometriosis and then has a child will often become cured with no treatment. Other risk factors for endometriosis include beginning menarche at an early age, having frequent menstrual cycles, and having periods that typically last more than seven days.

The amount of damage done by endometriosis depends on how bad a case the woman has, from mild cases to more severe ones. Endometriosis is a major cause of pain and infertility. Some women with very little of this tissue experience a lot of pain, while others with large masses feel nothing.

As with other conditions, it's important that you keep a list of all of your symptoms; the more information you give your doctor, the sooner he or she will arrive at the proper diagnosis. Many women with endometriosis often find that years go by before the source of their problems is pinpointed as endometriosis. Most doctors will first order tests, such as an ultrasound, although a laparoscopy—a procedure requiring the insertion of an instrument into the abdomen and looking at the pelvic organs—is usually necessary to make a definite diagnosis of endometriosis.

Many factors contribute to this lack of clarity in diagnosing endometriosis, but one that is under your control is not to consider any pain "normal" and to report it. It's understandable that you don't want to be considered a hypochondriac and may want to appear tough, but that only plays into the hands of this and many other diseases. Your doctor might not suspect endometriosis the first time you mention certain pains, but if you are still complaining a year later, and perhaps you never speak of any other pains, a pattern will develop that may lead to an earlier diagnosis. Even discussions with family members about your symptoms may be important because if several blood relations have similar problems, and you, in turn, report this to your doctor, this will point toward a condition that can be inherited, such as endometriosis.

Although no single cause has been found for endometriosis, the connection with estrogen is apparent, so the first line of treatment usually has to do with controlling the amount of estrogen in your body. If the pain is mild, over-the-counter pain relievers might be helpful. But if those or even prescription painkillers aren't effective and if you do not want to have children, then hormonal treatment may work. This would likely start with birth control pills, which will keep the endometrial tissue from filling with blood every month and growing. Other drugs that lower estrogen production are also effective. Of course, if you decide you want to get pregnant and go off these medications, then the symptoms of endometriosis will begin again.

The other route is surgery. How much surgery would be required depends on how widespread the endometrial cells are. If the disease is far enough advanced, only a complete hysterectomy will bring you the necessary relief, which makes any future pregnancies impossible.

Fighting a disease for which there really is no cure can be very frustrating and emotionally debilitating. There are support groups, and I strongly urge anyone with this disease to join one, in order to better cope.

Cervical Conditions

During the gynecological visit, a Pap test is usually performed. Cells from your cervix are scraped off and studied. It can be confusing to figure out the results of a Pap test. The system most widely used in the United States is the so-called Bethesda

Bethesda System for Pap Smears

Name	Meaning
Negative for intraepithelial lesion or malignancy	No sign of cancer or other cell anomaly
Atypical squamous cells	Unusual cells but not precancer or cancer
Atypical glandular cells	Abnormal cells that are of glandular origin
Low-grade squamous intraepithelial lesions	Very few cervical changes and HPV infection
High-grade squamous intraepithelial lesions	Precancer
Squamous cell carcinoma	Cancer

system. Above is a table with the various findings and their meanings.

If your result is normal, that means you have no abnormal cells on the cervix. An abnormal Pap test can mean there is an infection, precancerous cells, or other changes. Most abnormal results do not necessarily mean that there is cancer but instead indicate other changes. If you have an abnormal Pap test, you may need to have it repeated sooner, or you might need an additional test called a colposcopy, with a small cervical biopsy. Many times cell changes will disappear, or else there is treatment available to make sure the abnormal or precancerous cells don't become invasive cancerous cells. Normally, years will go by before the precancerous cells may become cancerous, although this can happen in less than a year. Most women who have invasive cancer of the cervix were not screened within the previous year, however, so going to the gynecologist for a Pap test does protect you from this type of cancer.

Most women with cervical cancer have few, if any, symptoms; that is why a regular Pap test is so important. The more advanced the cancer, the more likely that symptoms will become apparent, but advanced cervical cancer rarely, if ever, happens in women who have regular Pap tests. Among the possible symptoms of cervical cancer are abnormal bleeding, including bleeding between menstrual periods or after sexual intercourse, douching, or a pelvic exam; an increased vaginal discharge; pelvic pain, which can range from a dull ache to sharper pains and can be of short duration or long lasting; or pain during urination or in the bladder (usually this is a sign that the cancer has spread to other organs).

Again, it bears repeating that these symptoms could all signify some other medical condition or nothing at all, so don't go assuming that you have cancer if you exhibit any of these symptoms. On the other hand, don't ignore them, either, but go see your gynecologist to find out the actual cause.

Because cervical cancer has been shown to be linked to HPV (human papilloma virus), which is a sexually transmitted disease, the time to begin testing is when you first become sexually active. A woman who is twenty-one and not yet sexually active should also go to be tested, because a small percentage of all cervical cancers are not associated with HPV.

One statistic to remember with regard to cervical cancer is that the younger you begin to have intercourse and the more partners you have, the more likely you'll get infected with high-risk HPV and the greater your chances of developing cervical cancer. One reason for this is that the cervix of a teenager is still undergoing changes and thus is more vulnerable.

I know that young people today are not about to change their sexual habits because they fear getting cancer somewhere down the line. Fear tactics don't work because they fade away in the heat of passion. Yet it is important that we make our young people aware of the risks they run when they have too many sexual partners, especially at an early age. So many teens seem to think that because they can protect themselves against an unintended pregnancy and AIDS by using a condom, sex has few or no other repercussions. But sex still has serious consequences, and if teens are given the totality of all of the information, they may then come to a reasoned decision, rather than one made out of fear, and they might realize that waiting for the right person is the better course of action.

Ovarian Cancer

Ovarian cancer doesn't occur as often as other types of cancers that affect women, but because it rarely exhibits any typical symptoms, usually by the time it's discovered, it is at an advanced state, to the point of having spread to other organs, and so is more frequently fatal than cervical cancer. In fact, most ovarian cancers are detected after the cancer has already spread.

The most common symptom that a woman senses will be a feeling of abdominal bloating, which is created by fluid that collects in the abdomen. It may be misdiagnosed as something like irritable bowel syndrome. The one major difference to note is that while most digestive problems come and go, perhaps triggered by a certain type of food, the symptoms of ovarian cancer usually continue nonstop and gradually get worse. Because the cancer often grows in a direction that causes it to block the flow of urine, a combination of abdominal bloating and feelings of urinary urgency should be carefully examined by your doctor. Any sudden increase in girth, especially if this is not accompanied by any increase in eating (in fact, the woman may be eating less because of the discomfort), is also a symptom that should be taken seriously.

Is there anything you can do to avoid getting ovarian cancer if you have a genetic predisposition? Research seems to indicate that the more times you ovulate, the greater the chances of getting ovarian cancer. It's not clear whether the cancer may develop because of abnormalities created by the hormones released during ovulation or at the repair site after an egg is released from the ovary. In any case, anything you can do to prevent ovulation may be of help. That would include getting pregnant, breast-feeding, and taking oral contraceptives.

From Dr. Amos's Office: Ovarian Cancer

There has been some talk that women who take fertility drugs are at higher risk of developing ovarian cancer. Studies are not entirely clear about this, and because such women have had problems becoming pregnant, there may be other factors at work here. In any case, the odds of getting ovarian cancer are low, and if a woman wants to have a family and has been having problems conceiving or carrying a child, I believe that this particular risk, assuming it exists at all, should remain on the periphery of her decision making.

Other potential risk-increasing factors, beyond the purely genetic ones, include obesity and the taking of hormone replacement therapy (particularly estrogen) for more than five years.

Because the initial symptoms, bloating and digestive problems, may point you to another type of doctor at first, if that doctor suspects ovarian cancer and sends you to a gynecologist, you might consider going to a gynecological oncologist, a doctor who treats cancer in the reproductive organs, rather than going to your own gynecologist. A cancer specialist will be more likely to have the experience to ascertain whether ovarian cancer may be the cause of your symptoms.

Endometrial Cancer

Endometrial cancer is cancer that develops in the endometrium, which is the inside lining of the uterus (cancer that develops in the muscle tissue is called sarcoma of the uterus). Endometrial cancer most often strikes older, postmenopausal women. It is a slow-moving cancer, and usually the first observable symptom of this cancer is irregular bleeding, which is particularly noticeable in postmenopausal women. Pelvic pain and abnormal vaginal discharge are also symptoms. There were about forty-two thousand cases of this cancer in 2009, of which seven thousand resulted in death.

Your body secretes two hormones that regulate your menstrual period, estrogen and progesterone. Estrogen stimulates the growth of the endometrial tissue, and if the balance between the two hormones

From Dr. Amos's Office: Endometrial Cancer

If you're taking tamoxifen to combat breast cancer, this puts you at a higher risk of developing endometrial cancer. That's not to say that you shouldn't continue to take tamoxifen but only that you need to undergo a regular gynecologic exam. A Pap test detects cervical cancer, and it will not routinely reveal endometrial cancer. A biopsy of the tissue of the endometrium is needed, which means that either a small, flexible tube will be inserted into the uterus via the cervix to scrape off some cells or else a D&C (dilation and curettage) will be performed, in which the doctor will use a curette (a spoon-shaped instrument) to remove tissue.

This cancer is stimulated by continued contact with estrogen, the female hormone that is produced by the ovaries. Yet estrogen is also produced by fat cells, so women who are overweight are prone to developing this form of cancer. Women who are between 25 and 50 pounds overweight triple their risk, while heavier women increase their risk factor tenfold.

Can coffee protect you from getting endometrial cancer? Some research has shown that drinking at least two cups of coffee a day does seem to have a preventive effect, especially among obese women. Coffee may affect estrogen production, which may be how it protects against this type of cancer. Yet this link has not been proved, and you'd be better off losing as much weight as possible for the overall health benefits this would offer, rather than relying on coffee to protect you.

Anything that extends the production of estrogen is thought to be a risk factor for endometrial cancer, so that a woman who starts menarche early or goes through menopause later is at greater risk. Although your body produces more estrogen when you are pregnant, it is believed that pregnancy lowers the chances of getting endometrial cancer, perhaps because pregnancy also increases the level of progesterone, and it is the balance of the two that counts. Also, if you have any irregularities with regard to ovulation, so that you miss ovulating in some months, that exposes you to greater amounts of estrogen and so is a risk factor. (Obese women tend to skip ovulating more often than thinner women do.)

Another condition, polycystic ovary syndrome, also causes women not to ovulate every month. There are other risk factors as well, including a hereditary tendency and having had other cancers, such as ovarian or cervical cancer.

changes so that estrogen dominates, this may cause abnormal cell growth to proliferate, leading to the development of cancer.

Because the main symptom is abnormal bleeding and most women who get this form of cancer are old enough to have gone through menopause, this bleeding is quickly apparent as a sign that something is wrong. One of the likely scenarios is endometrial cancer, so if a woman reports this abnormal bleeding to her doctor as quickly as possible, instead of waiting for her yearly checkup, for example, then the odds of surviving endometrial cancer are very good.

Other symptoms include pelvic pain, pain after intercourse, bleeding in between periods for women who have not yet gone through menopause, an abnormal vaginal discharge, and unexpected weight loss. Of course, any of these symptoms could be the sign of something else, but because it is important to catch endometrial cancer at the earliest possible stage, it is better to assume the worst and go right to your doctor than to wait for an extended period of time to see if the symptoms go away on their own.

Breast Cancer

The two words *breast cancer* strike fear in most women, especially if they've heard the statistic that one woman in eight will get breast cancer.

The American Cancer Society's most recent estimates for breast cancer in the United States predict that in 2011:

- About 230,480 new cases of invasive breast cancer will be diagnosed in women
- About 57,650 new cases of carcinoma in situ (CIS) will be diagnosed (CIS is noninvasive and is the earliest form of breast cancer)
- About 39,520 women will die from breast cancer

Breast cancer tends to strike both younger and older women, and the older you are, the greater your risk, but if you are a young woman, say age twenty-five, the odds of your getting breast cancer in the next ten years are 1 in 2,500. Whatever the statistics, though, breast cancer remains a disease that makes most women fearful, in part because even if one survives, and the likelihood of that is good, the loss of a breast is much more apparent than the loss of an inner organ, and because one's breasts are closely tied to one's sense of self-worth, mere survival can still leave one a true victim to breast cancer.

When it comes to breast cancer, there is a big controversy taking place about whether it is worthwhile for a woman to get a mammogram, or a breast X-ray. Rather than wait to discuss this issue later in this chapter, because it is so controversial, I am going to deal with it right up front. I wish I could do this in a simple way, but this is not a simple issue.

First off, you need to know what a mammogram is. A mammogram is a breast X-ray that can locate abnormalities inside your breast and, to a certain extent, determine whether they are benign or cancerous. If you've never gone for a breast X-ray, I wouldn't want to hide from you the fact that it's not the most pleasant of experiences, because your breast gets squeezed between two metal plates—it's uncomfortable and may even hurt a bit. Yet it's not so uncomfortable that this should prevent you from going. Nor should you avoid it because you're embarrassed about having your breast manipulated by a technician. If, however, you *and your doctor* feel that going for a mammogram is not necessary, then you may continue to avoid this experience.

Today you also have a choice of mammograms. With the original mammogram, which is still widely used because it is the most cost effective, the picture comes out on film. Yet modern technology has developed the digital mammogram, which offers a more detailed look and can be sent to another doctor for examination quite easily. Not every practitioner has access to this equipment, and it's unclear whether the extra cost is justified, but the added question of whether you need the most modern mammogram adds to the complexity of the decision.

Because there are various types of breast cancer, some more aggressive than others, along with different types of breasts, some with denser tissue than others, and because of the wide disparity in the ages of women, I can't give you one answer on whether going for a mammogram is likely to save your life or just make it miserable. That's why the American Cancer Society has questioned the overall value of mammograms.

Let's start with the effectiveness of mammograms. In a woman with dense breasts—in other words, with a lot of fatty tissue—a mammogram is more likely to miss tumors. On the other hand, it may pick up tumors that are not life threatening but that once discovered will lead to treatment that will forever change the woman's life and self-image, if she undergoes surgery, radiation, and/or chemotherapy.

If you're asking yourself right now, "How dense is my breast?" the ironic answer is that the only way to ascertain that information is by having a mammogram. Yet this turns out to be important information. Most of the time when you get the result of your mammogram, it's either positive or negative, and nothing is mentioned about your breast density. So if you didn't know to ask about this fact before, now you know that if you go for a mammogram, you should ask about your breast density. Once you know this, you can at least factor it into your decision making in the future.

One thing you do know is your age. If you are younger than fifty, don't smoke, and don't have a genetic tendency toward breast cancer, meaning you don't have a lot of relatives (and it's better to have no relatives) who have had the disease, you could make the decision to skip having mammograms. If you are older than sixty, you might also make the identical decision, though in both of these instances I strongly urge you not to decide without consulting your gynecologist. As I said, the issues are complicated, and you really want to ensure that you make the right decision.

Because older women are stricken by breast cancer more often, why would an older woman even consider not going for a mammogram? Because the type of cancer that usually occurs in an older woman is the slow-growing kind, and you're much more likely to die of another cause (heart attack, other type of cancer, and so on) before this type of breast cancer kills you, so why go through the torture of knowing you have breast cancer and possibly that knowledge leading you to have all sorts of serious treatments that you might not really need?

What about if you're between fifty and sixty? It's your decision, but I would recommend that you go for a yearly mammography. This test will not guard you against breast cancer entirely, especially if you have dense breasts, but it could pick up a dangerous cancer and save your life, making it the wiser choice for women in this age bracket.

Yes, this whole issue is confusing, and by the time you read this, more studies may have come out that will only add to the confusion. Despite all of the conflicting views, the best advice is to stay as informed as possible and discuss everything with your gynecologist. Together, the two of you should be able to map out a game plan that will be the right one for you. Of course, if you feel safer going for a yearly mammogram, whatever your age, then go. No matter what your decision, you should definitely give yourself a monthly self-examination to feel for any lumps. Lumps may not pose any danger, but if there is one, then you absolutely must see a doctor.

I'm not a medical doctor, so when it comes to any of these medical issues in which the medical opinions go back and forth, I'm just as confused as you are. What's my solution? Find the very best doctor that you can, and then rely on his or her opinion. Finding the best doctor is under your control. Ask the people you know whom you trust to be careful about getting the best possible medical care. Some of these people may be wealthier than you, but when it comes to your health, that's one time you shouldn't count pennies. Ask other doctors for referrals to specialists. Do your homework. Once you've settled on a doctor you feel you can trust, if you don't want to spend hundreds of hours studying medical websites, then you can simply allow this doctor to decide. Yet even if you do keep up with the latest news, when you talk with your doctor, you'll have the confidence that what you're hearing is coming from someone who really knows what he or she is talking about.

Breast Examination

The first line of defense against breast cancer is literally in your hands. A monthly breast self-exam (BSE) can detect signs of breast cancer in between your yearly visit to the gynecologist (see the illustration in the appendix). You should ask your gynecologist to show you how to do one during your next visit, if you haven't been given that information before.

Some women might ask, "What if my breasts are always lumpy?" The reason it is important for you to do a monthly breast exam is to become familiar with your breasts, including how they feel. Suppose you've been to the gynecologist, and he or she has examined your breasts and found them fine and has taught you how to examine them and what your normal breasts should feel like. Then you examine them yourself and feel some lumps, but now you know that you don't have to worry about those because they're of the "normal" variety. It is also normal for your breasts to develop some lumps at various times of the month. When you're having your period, your breasts may become tender, sore, and swollen. You may also find that your breasts appear more lumpy. That's because your breasts accumulate fluid during your period. These lumps should go away after your period ends. If they do not, contact your doctor.

If you ever feel a lump in one breast at some time when it's not your period, the first thing you should check is your other breast. If there's a similar lump there, then it's something you can note and tell your doctor about later, but there's no rush. Yet if a lump of any size appears when you're not having your period and there is no lump in the corresponding spot in your other breast, you should report that to your doctor. Don't panic, because 80 percent of such lumps are not cancerous, but don't ignore it either.

Surviving Breast Cancer

If you do learn that you have breast cancer, the one emotion you probably can never imagine feeling is gratitude. Shock, fear, anger—these are more normal reactions. Yet you can also feel grateful for living in these modern times, when the breast cancer survival rate is so high. Medical science has enormously improved your odds of living a full and healthy life, after you overcome cancer.

Fighting cancer is a battle, and like any battle, it's easier if you have support. That feeling of working together with others to fight your cancer will give you a major psychological advantage. Think of the medical professionals who help with your treatment as your own personal "get-well" team. You may also want to join a cancer support group, whose members are going through similar struggles. Even if your friends and family rally around you, they cannot fathom what you are experiencing, yet a total stranger who is also a cancer survivor can. If you are in a romantic relationship or married, your partner may have many intense, unspoken, or even conflicting feelings about your illness. Ideally, you want and expect your partner to be endlessly patient and supportive through all of your emotional upheavals and night terrors. In the real world, however, people are human. Your partner may hide behind a wall of silence, unwilling to admit how much he is afraid to lose you. He may feel anger at the possibility that you will "desert" him by dying or may get annoyed at being thrust into the role of caretaker. In addition, sometimes one or both partners in a couple look at the woman's body after cancer treatment as something (and I'm sorry to use such a strong word) repugnant. The woman might feel as if her breasts are no longer appealing, the man may feel that way, or they both could feel that way. It's a common reaction, and although it can be overcome, it takes an effort on the part of both people. In this case, having sex may actually be part of the treatment as it gives you an added incentive. And once you start having sex three or four times a week, both of you will be much less likely to want to stop. You'll have gotten over any squeamishness, and that will go a long way toward ensuring that your sex life remains healthy throughout this battle against cancer.

Dyspareunia

Another topic that women bring up with their gynecologists is painful sex, which in the medical world is called dyspareunia. As with any pain, sometimes the condition can be mild so that it's only after sex that the woman notices some soreness, or else the pain could be so severe that the woman cannot have intercourse at all. In the former case, the solution is often a medical one, while in the latter, although medical attention can sometimes be offered, the problem is often more psychological in nature.

Vaginal pain during intercourse could have many different sources, such as certain medical conditions or simply not having enough lubrication, because of either medical or psychological issues.

Vaginal Lubrication

Vaginal lubrication is created through the production of fluid from inside the vagina by glands such as the Bartholin's and the Skene's glands. The Skene's gland, especially, is thought to be the source for female ejaculation. (As an aside, the Skene's gland was named after Dr. Alexander Skene, who at the end of the nineteenth century worked at the same hospital in Brooklyn where Dr. Amos trained.)

Occasionally, a woman has medical problems that can lead to less or no production of fluid by these glands, and that's something your doctor will look into and, if possible, correct.

Even when there are no medical issues, not having enough vaginal lubrication can happen if the couple doesn't engage in enough foreplay to the woman so that she gets sufficiently aroused to start the flow of lubrication. Notice that I said "the couple." Although it's true that it's the man's job to perform foreplay, it's up to the woman to let him know when she's ready to have intercourse. If she doesn't speak up and tell him that she needs more foreplay, and he's raring to go, then intercourse may begin before she's ready, and she'll wind up in pain afterward. So the very first step in dealing with this sort of pain is to make sure that the two partners are communicating with each other about their sex life.

Why is it the woman's fault at all? Shouldn't her male partner be able to tell whether she's sufficiently lubricated? Even though many men can tell, the actual answer to that question is no. Because even if a man is an expert lover and he is certain that his partner is ready for intercourse, it's still just a guess on his part. Only the woman can really know how aroused she feels. Perhaps there is enough lubrication, but she's a little distracted and simply not yet ready to begin intercourse. Since he can't read her mind, she has to be the one to give him the signal. The bottom line is, the woman has to remain in control when it comes to deciding when she is actually ready to have intercourse.

More often, the reason for her lack of arousal is that even though she may love her partner, something is taking place in their relationship that causes resentment on her part, or events outside of the relationship, such as problems at work, are preventing her from becoming fully aroused. Without that arousal, she won't produce enough lubrication.

If there's a serious relationship problem, the couple should go for counseling to try to resolve matters. Yet very often, there is no psychological block that prevents the woman from desiring to have sex with her partner. In that case, the couple should use an artificial lubricant.

The first artificial lubricant was probably saliva. Since it contains mucus, it's naturally slippery. Yet because it's mostly made up of water, and the water dries out, it loses its lubricating effects rather quickly, so is not a good option.

Before there were commercially available lubricants for sex, many people turned to natural substances such as butter or olive oil. These oily substances retain their lubricating properties, so that makes them good for the job. Oils don't mix with water, however, so you can't clean oil off your body without using soap. The drawback is that using soap to clean the inside of a vagina will also destroy the vagina's own environment, the vagina's so-called flora, and this can lead to infection. If you don't clean all of the oil out of the vagina, it creates a good place for bacteria to breed, which can lead to more problems. So the bottom line is, don't go to the kitchen when looking for lubrication but instead head for the drugstore or the sex shop.

There's a vast array of products sold as sexual lubricants. Some are water based, some petroleum based, and others silicone based. Because both the petroleum-based and the silicone-based lubricants are hard to clean, and because petroleum-based lubricants can destroy the latex in condoms (and very quickly), the only type of lubricants I recommend are the water-based ones. Some of these also include flavors and aromas, and if they add to your pleasure, feel free to use them, but the simple varieties work fine.

The problem with water-based lubricants is that they do dry out after a while, so just because you applied the lubricant once doesn't mean that you're still protected if you're having sex fifteen minutes later. Sometimes adding a little water will restore the lubricant's effectiveness (assuming you're on a tight budget), but otherwise you can just add some more lubricant. The best way to apply a lubricant, by the way, is simply to spread it on the male's erect penis. Once there, it will be easily introduced all the way into the vagina, where it needs to work.

Some women ask why they seem to get yeast infections when they use a water-based lubricant. The answer is that some water-based lubricants contain glycerin. Glycerin is sweet, so it can make your vagina a good breeding ground for microbes. If you encounter this problem, check the labels carefully and find a water-based lubricant that doesn't contain glycerin.

From Dr. Amos's Office: Melissa and Bob's Story

A couple came to see me because they were having difficulties getting pregnant. They had been trying for fourteen months without success. I reviewed the woman's history (she had a regular thirty-day menstrual cycle, which indicated ovulation), and we performed a sperm count, which was fine. They were making love regularly, two to three times a week; however, in asking about lubricants, they told me they were using a common petroleum-based lubricant, which after review has been found to kill sperm. I recommended that they engage in more foreplay before sexual intercourse and if necessary use a more sperm-friendly lubricant. Six weeks later, they called to tell me that their pregnancy test was positive.

What about couples who have difficulties conceiving? It's been shown that the ingredients in artificial lubricants can slow down the sperm's ability to swim, and they can actually kill sperm and could be a factor in decreasing your chances of conceiving. Because many couples who face these problems end up making love on particular dates of the calendar, that pressure alone can make it harder for the woman to become aroused and therefore increases her need for an artificial lubricant. The solution is to use a lubricant that doesn't have this negative effect on sperm. Pre-Seed has been given FDA approval to make the claim that it is safe to use for couples trying to conceive.

Medical Reasons for Dyspareunia

Not all pain suffered by women during intercourse comes from a lack of lubrication. Other potential causes of pain during sex include infections of the vagina (vaginitis), which can be caused by one or more organisms (such as chlamydia, gonorrhea, herpes, trichomoniasis, or a yeast infection); structural problems of the uterus or the vagina, such as a tipped uterus, which means she feels pain each time her partner's penis comes into contact with her cervix; allergies, including an allergy to the latex in a condom or other contraceptive and sometimes even to the man's penis or his ejaculate; endometriosis (endometrial lining outside the uterus); infections of the ovaries or the fallopian tubes; ovarian cysts or tumors; urinary tract infections; interstitial cystitis; and scarring of the vagina and the perineum, such as from the effects of childbirth. One important condition that's associated with pain during sex is an ectopic pregnancy, a pregnancy that's outside the uterus, usually in one of the fallopian tubes. If you have pain during sex and you could be pregnant, it's important to let your doctor know as soon as possible. Your doctor can do some tests, such as a sonogram, to make sure the pregnancy is in the right place.

Only if your gynecologist knows you have a problem with painful intercourse can she or he diagnose what is wrong and come up with a potential solution so that you can begin to enjoy pain-free sex. Pain during intercourse is not normal, and it's important that you let your doctor know whenever you feel pain at this time.

Psychological Reasons for Dyspareunia

Another major cause of pain is psychological in nature. Some women unconsciously tighten their vaginal muscles, making penetration either painful or actually impossible. This condition is called vaginismus. The woman may love her partner and may want to have sex, but something in her subconscious is stopping her from allowing this to happen. Such a reaction could stem from a past psychological trauma, such as rape or incest. Or else it could have to do with the woman's upbringing. If she was told over and over again that sex was dirty and not to be enjoyed, then no matter how much she wants to enjoy it now, she might not be able to overcome her upbringing, at least not by herself. Sometimes a relationship issue shows itself in this way. Very often, vaginismus occurs when two people first attempt to have sex, although sometimes it develops later in life. Or maybe a woman who has always been able to enjoy sex with other partners might encounter this problem with a new partner, which may or may not have something to do with him or that relationship.

From Dr. Amos's Office: Vaginismus

Tightening of the muscles surrounding the vagina is something that every gynecologist encounters from time to time while conducting the pelvic exam. Some women are so nervous about it that they can't stop themselves from tightening their vaginal muscles, so that it is impossible to insert the speculum or the finger. These women may or may not also have this problem when trying to have intercourse.

There are two approaches to dealing with vaginismus. Generally, the first one that is employed is the psychological, because, after all, the underlying cause is psychological. The woman would be sent to a psychologist, a sex therapist, or another counselor, and the professional would try to determine the source of the problem. If that can be discovered, then the counselor might be able to help the woman overcome it by talking to her, explaining what is going on, and then getting her to learn to relax her muscles. In general, her partner should also be seen, because they will have to work closely together to make progress. Depending on the severity, the couple might be able to engage in intercourse right away, even if to a limited degree, or else more time might be needed to get her to learn how to relax those muscles.

In some cases, the mental block is so strong that the woman cannot help herself, even with professional assistance. In such cases, she will be sent back to the gynecologist, who will give her a series of dilators of varying sizes. The woman would then work at trying to get the smallest inside her vagina first, perhaps with the doctor's help the initial time and further repetitions at home, and would slowly progress to a larger and larger size. This method usually will eventually lead to a point where her vagina will be large enough to allow intercourse.

Dealing with Sexual Problems

Any time that a couple is dealing with pain during intercourse, they should consider all other options for getting sexual satisfaction that are at their disposal. As I already pointed out, most women cannot have an orgasm from intercourse alone, so many couples may already be engaging in other forms of sex, including masturbation and oral sex, in order to help the woman have an orgasm. If intercourse is not possible for a length of time, then those same methods should be used by both partners to please each other. It's certainly frustrating when you cannot share having intercourse, but that doesn't have to result in complete sexual frustration. If each partner is willing to give the other sexual release using other means, then their relationship should not suffer any damage during the time they are dealing with painful intercourse. The same is true at any other time when sexual intercourse is either not possible or not practical, for example, during the latter months of pregnancy, when an injury makes intercourse difficult (such as a back injury to one partner), and so on.

A situation faced by many couples is that one or the other develops a health problem that may appear to make sex more risky. This is something more likely to be encountered by older couples, but it can occur at almost any age. For example, if one partner has had a heart attack or a stroke, that person or his or her partner may be hesitant to have sex out of the fear that doing so would cause another heart attack or stroke. Now, in this particular example, the patient's doctor is supposed to give the patient instructions on what is and is not permitted. Yet oftentimes those instructions aren't clear enough. The main reason, again, is that doctors are often not given sufficient training in sexual issues, plus they are likely to have their own inhibitions in talking about sex. If, however, the woman has a good relationship with her gynecologist regarding sexual matters, having spoken of them regularly over the years, then it would certainly be appropriate to ask her gynecologist to speak with the specialist, such as a cardiologist or a neurologist, to find out exactly what sexual activity is and is not allowed. Hearing your doctor give the explanation and being able to ask questions of someone you already talk to about sexual matters may make receiving and absorbing the information a lot easier.

The same advice applies when a medication causes problems in the sexual arena. If a doctor prescribes a medication for another condition, such as diabetes or depression, and that medicine disrupts your sex life, yet you don't feel comfortable talking to your doctor about it, and it's easier for you to talk to your gynecologist, then ask your gynecologist to intervene. Very often a different drug, which is equally effective at treating the original condition, will not have the same side effects when it comes to sex. So if the two doctors communicate, hopefully you can be put on another drug that will not damage your sex life.

Male Dyspareunia

Painful intercourse is not the exclusive domain of women; it can also happen in men. Male dyspareunia can happen from pain in the bladder, the testes, the prostate, or even the rectum. The dyspareunia can be experienced either during sex or during ejaculation. Again, the gynecologist may be the only doctor the couple has with whom sex is discussed, so their gynecologist could be a great source of help.

6

Avoiding Pregnancy

Although the original purpose of sex was to cause pregnancy, these days most sexual activity is for pleasure only. In this chapter, you'll learn how to make sure that you don't become pregnant—unless, of course, you want to!

The concept of women's liberation may be widely considered a change in the political status of women. Yet the most significant occurrence that liberated women was the advent of the birth control pill, which gave women control over whether they would become pregnant. Once women could have sexual relations without having to worry about unintended pregnancies, they truly started to become the equals of men. And, of course, it is your gynecologist, not an elected official, who offers you the key to this particular form of freedom.

Many young women first come into contact with a gynecologist to obtain a prescription for birth control pills. This may seem like a routine matter, to both the young women and their gynecologists, but in fact it sets the tone for this important relationship. If a woman says to herself, "I need to get on the pill, so it doesn't matter which gynecologist I see," she is making a mistake. Her relationship with her gynecologist should be personal and long lasting, but if she starts out seeing a gynecologist without giving much thought to her choice of doctor, she may never establish the type of relationship that will be the most productive for her.

The first gynecologists whom many women see are the ones their mothers go to. That's not necessarily a bad start, but it can have some drawbacks. Although the doctor-patient relationship is always a private one, a young woman may assume that if she tells her mother's doctor too much, some of the information may somehow get back to her mother, so she maintains a wall of secrecy between herself and this doctor. As I've showed you again and again in this book, that is a big mistake. Because it may be impossible for a young woman to fully trust her mother's doctor, she might be better off seeking out her own doctor, in whom she can have full confidence when it comes to maintaining her privacy.

Young people who engage in sexual relations that they keep secret from their parents will naturally distrust all adults. When

---

From Dr. Amos's Office: Your Own Gynecologist

If ten years have gone by and you're still seeing your mother's gynecologist, yet you don't feel that the rapport between the two of you is good, I would suggest that you look for your own gynecologist. It is difficult to change a relationship, of any kind, and that includes the one you have with your gynecologist. If you start seeing a new gynecologist, you can prepare yourself ahead of time to make sure that this new relationship will be as open as necessary to provide you with the best possible health care. Don't worry about hurting the feelings of your old gynecologist or be concerned about what your mother will say. The relationship between you and your gynecologist is an important one, so you needn't stick with a gynecologist with whom you don't feel you can talk openly and honestly.

you're keeping a secret of any sort, you tend to be a little paranoid. My recommendation to a young woman who is seeing her mother's doctor is to bring up the issue of privacy right away. Hearing the doctor confirm that nothing that she says will get back to her mother should allow open communications to develop.

Preventing Pregnancy and Disease

Though I've discussed preventing disease in the previous chapter, in many cases the two issues are combined because of the use of condoms. Maybe, for whatever reason, condoms are the best option for you to prevent pregnancy, but I urge you to separate the two issues when deciding which type of contraception to choose. Every health practitioner recommends condom usage to prevent disease because it's really the only option. We all know that condoms can break or fall off, so they're far from perfect, but in the case of many STDs we sadly have no other form of protection to offer patients. The failure rate of condoms also applies to preventing pregnancy, so many women find themselves using condoms for disease prevention and another form of protection against unintended pregnancies. That's not overkill but rather a very prudent approach and an issue you need to discuss with your doctor.

Condoms

A condom is a sheath, usually made of latex, though it could also be made of silicone or lambskin, that covers the penis so that when a man ejaculates during intercourse, his sperm are not deposited inside the vagina. There are two types of condom use: perfect and typical. If used perfectly, condoms offer very effective protection, resulting in an approximately 2 percent pregnancy rate per year. Yet that word *perfectly* is the problem. The typical use of condoms is more the norm, and it results in about a

10 to 18 percent pregnancy rate per year. Many men complain that they don't like using condoms. If a man can prove to a woman that he is disease-free (hopefully, by passing a medical test and not just by sweet talking her into believing him), then during the woman's "safe" times, he might try to convince her that the condom is not needed. But the "safe" period is far from 100 percent safe. There's no guarantee when the ovaries will release an egg. Some women even release an egg shortly after the end of their period. Other women who are normally as regular as clock-work suddenly ovulate at a different time. And sperm can survive up to five to six days inside a woman's uterus, so if she ovulates within that time frame, there is a chance she will get pregnant. There is no actual "safe" period if you want to protect yourself 100 percent. Therefore, if you are using condoms, you must use them 100 percent of the time. Yet because so many people do skip using them, their overall efficacy drops.

Another risk is that condoms can break or fall off. They can be put on incorrectly (see the illustration in the appendix). If both of you are careful, condoms are effective—but this means that you use the right-size condoms (they come in as many as seventy different sizes) and then take every precaution when removing the condom (holding the top so that there can be no leakage). Again, though, if you've had a drink or two, will you be as protected as you should be?

Many men complain about using condoms. Part of this is undoubtedly that they're ashamed of having to go to the drugstore to buy them, or they don't want to spend the money. Yet there's probably some truth to the complaint that having intercourse with a condom doesn't feel quite the same as without one. If you're a woman who suspects that your partner is either too shy or too cheap to purchase his own condoms, then you need to buy them and see if that stops his whining about them. If that doesn't work and you're not 100 percent certain that you're not at risk of getting a sexually transmitted disease, then my advice is to move on. You can catch a disease, not even know it, and end up unable to have children when you want to. Your health is too important to risk, so never have unprotected sex.

If you're married and having a baby wouldn't be the end of the world, then condoms are fine. If you're not ready to have a baby and an unintended pregnancy would be a calamity, relying only on condoms could be a big mistake. That's not to say you shouldn't use condoms for disease protection, just not as your only means of birth control if protection against an unintended pregnancy is very important to you. If you're in that category, what are your other options?

The Pill

Tens of millions of sexually active women take an oral contraceptive, otherwise known as the birth control pill, every day (or for at least three out of four weeks a month) and are protected against an unintended pregnancy. The pill is a very effective method of preventing pregnancy, but you may be surprised to learn that we don't know 100 percent how the pill works. We believe that the pill prevents your ovaries from releasing an egg every month, but we're not sure that happens every month. We also know that the pill keeps your cervical mucus from thinning out as it is supposed to do during your fertile period, and that prevents sperm from penetrating the cervix and meeting up with an egg. The pill may also prevent a sperm from attaching itself to an egg and may keep a fertilized egg from attaching itself to the womb to develop into a baby. Therefore, we don't know for certain whether the pill works via one of the previous methods or a combination of all four of them. Yet since the development of the pill in 1960, the one thing we do know is that women who take it (or use a similar device— more on that in a moment) rarely become pregnant. How rarely? If the pill is used perfectly, fewer than 1 in 300 women will get pregnant during one year's time, while under typical use that rate is closer to 5 percent. Reasons for the pill not being as effective include mistakes made by women taking the pill, interference with other medications, and the woman's body not absorbing enough of the pill (for example, if a woman vomits or has diarrhea). Recently, a published study showed that obese women (starting with a BMI or body mass index of 27.3) who take the pill are more likely to get pregnant. The reasons for that are not completely understood, but in general, the odds of not getting pregnant while on the pill are pretty good.

I've been saying "the pill," which might make it sound as if there is only one pill, but in fact that there are many from which to choose, in terms of both type and brand. All birth control pills contain hormones. Combination pills contain both estrogen and progestin, while "mini-pills" contain only progestin. Ever since the pill first came out, the doses of the hormones have been lowered so that the risks from any side effects have been significantly reduced. This lowering has also decreased the level of protection, but so marginally that given the lesser risks, overall this has been a benefit to women's health.

The Risks

If you follow the news at all, you're probably aware that the risks and benefits of the pill seem to change with some regularity. First, researchers announce that it protects women against one form of cancer, then another study indicates that it increases the risk for something else. That's why you have to ask your doctor about whether the pill is safe for you. Your doctor knows all about your entire medical history and can then recommend the safest pill for you or tell you that the risks are too great altogether (which generally applies to women older than thirty-five who smoke). Admittedly, this is not a decision to be taken lightly because of the potential dangers, but you also have to consider that giving birth involves a risk, too, so protecting yourself against getting pregnant may outweigh the other risks. Despite whatever you read in the media, the decision about whether to use the pill has to be an individual one, because of the state of your overall health, and the only person who can truly help you make that decision is your doctor.

Other Side Effects

So far, I've mentioned risks of serious consequence, but a woman can experience other side effects from taking the pill that, while not serious, can be annoying, such as occasional spotting, mild nausea, breast tenderness and/or enlargement, and a slight weight gain. Usually, any such side effects will disappear after a few months as her body adjusts to the increased hormone levels.

Some women discover that when fully protected against pregnancy by the pill, this new confidence increases their desire for sex, while others find that the change in their hormones decreases their desire for sex. If the latter happens, you might change the dosage of the pill you are taking; try a different method of using hormones, such as a shot or a vaginal ring (see further on for more details); or switch to another method entirely.

There's a French saying, "*l'appetit vient on mangeant*," which translates as "the appetite arrives while eating," and this concept can apply to sex as well. If you start taking the pill and find that your desire for sex decreases, try making love anyway, despite that initial lack of desire, and there's a good chance that after some cuddling and foreplay, your level of arousal will suddenly rise. Don't assume that just because you're not feeling in the mood when you start that you won't be glad you had sex by the time you're finished.

There are now birth control pills that also stop you from having your period altogether. Considering the pet names women have given to their menstrual period (such as "the curse"), you might consider this a positive side effect. You should definitely talk about this option with your health-care provider to make sure that any additional risks don't outweigh this one benefit. Because these pills are relatively new, we don't know the potential long-term effects.

If and when you decide that the time has come to get pregnant, you should be able to do so simply by no longer taking your daily pill. Some women's natural hormone levels take longer than others' to stabilize so that they are once again capable of becoming pregnant, but in most cases a month or two should do the trick. Most women start ovulating and having a regular period again within one to two months after stopping the pill.

Other Options

You have other options besides the condom and the pill to protect yourself against unwanted pregnancy. Others that also involve the use of hormones include

- **Depo-Provera**. Depo-Provera is a shot of hormones that lasts for three months. For women who think they might forget to take a pill every day, this method may provide a good alternative, although, of course, you must visit your doctor every twelve weeks to get the next shot. The side effects can include heavier-than-normal bleeding, a complete cessation of menses, or spotting. One drawback to this method is that it can take a long time to get pregnant, even after the three months are up.

- **Birth Control Patch**. Using a patch to deliver the hormones for protection against an unintended pregnancy is a good method for women who don't want to see their doctor every three months for a shot but are also afraid that they might not remember to take a daily pill. Yet if you forget to change your patch after a week, you'll be doing the same thing as not taking a pill. The risks for the patch are about the same as for the other methods that use hormones.

- **Vaginal Ring**. With this method, you place a ring with hormones into your vagina for three weeks. It's not a complicated process, although occasionally the ring falls out, which could leave you unprotected. The risks are the same as for the other hormonal methods.

Methods without any hormones include

- **Intrauterine Device (IUD)**. The IUD is one of the most popular methods of birth control in the world, although you would never know that if you lived in the United States. In the mid-1970s, there were serious problems with one brand of IUD, which had a design error with its string. The negative publicity significantly decreased IUD use in the United States, which remains at about 2 percent of all contraceptive methods. That particular IUD was immediately taken off the market, and the existing IUDs are safe, effective, and cheap

    There are two general types of IUD. The classic IUD contains copper, which prevents the sperm from attaching itself to an egg. These IUDs can be left in place and are effective for up to ten years. Some newer IUDs include a low dose of hormones, so that in addition to preventing pregnancy, they also can lessen a woman's period in terms of flow or stop it altogether.

    IUDs are very effective, more effective than the pill, and only one in a hundred women using an IUD will become pregnant. They have few side effects and, once in place, require no action on the part of the woman, other than to check every once in a while to see if the string is in place, proving that the IUD is still there. Some men claim that they can feel the string and that it is annoying, but that's not usually the case.

From Dr. Amos's Office: Vanessa's Story

One of my patients wanted to use a method of birth control for about three years and wanted to be able to get pregnant right after she stopped using it. I recommended an IUD because, unlike after the pill, when it can take a woman several months to start ovulating again, it is possible to get pregnant as soon as the IUD has been removed. Three years later, she asked me to remove the IUD, and lo and behold, she became pregnant within two weeks.

Other Nonhormonal Methods

There are other methods that people use to prevent pregnancy. Some are used by very few women, such as the diaphragm, which was once popular but has now gone out of style, and the cervical cap and the female condom. The IUD is also unpopular in the United States, but it is a good method that has clear advantages, which is why I discussed it at length in the previous section. The diaphragm, the cervical cap, and the female condom don't share those advantages, so I'm not going to say much more about them.

Withdrawal

One popular method of birth control is called the withdrawal or pull-out method. What it means is that the man withdraws his penis from the vagina right before he is going to ejaculate. It's too bad that this is a popular method because it has serious drawbacks. The first is the possibility that there can be sperm in the pre-ejaculatory fluid, secreted by the Cowper's gland, the purpose of which is to act as a lubricant for the ejaculate. There could be sperm left over in the man's penis from the last time he ejaculated that could be picked up and left inside the woman. The odds aren't great that this will happen, but it could. And, of course, some men either believe they can withdraw in time and fail to do so, or they say they will withdraw and have no intentions of doing so. In other words, with this method the woman is at the mercy of the man. For that reason, I don't recommend using the withdrawal method. In addition, this method offers no protection whatsoever against sexually transmitted diseases.

Natural Family Planning

Earlier, I spoke about people who have unprotected sex during the woman's "safe" period, and I indicated that this doesn't work because what might appear to be safe (that is, a window where the woman cannot get pregnant) might end up not being safe because when a woman releases an egg, she does not always follow a strict timetable. Natural family planning takes this method several steps further by having the woman monitor her bodily functions in several key ways, including measuring her body temperature every morning before she gets out of bed. Ovulation does cause certain changes in a woman's body, and by carefully looking for these signs, a woman can prevent an unintended pregnancy. In fact, many women use the same methods to become pregnant when they are having difficulties.

Can this method be used effectively to prevent pregnancy? Yes, but it takes a lot of work. You have to be really motivated, and it's not totally effective because, as I've said several times, a woman's body can do something unexpected. Then there's also the question of what this method does to your sex life. Assuming you have chosen this method so that you can avoid using any artificial method of birth control, then that means you can have sex only at certain times, so spontaneity is completely removed from the equation. This means both partners have to be committed to using this method. To be clear, the people who adopt this method are usually religious and do so if they don't want to use artificial birth control because it is forbidden by their religion, but they also don't want to have children. If this is the only method that their religion permits, then that's what they should use. Yet using this method without being strengthened by one's religious beliefs is difficult.

Many women who are breast-feeding count on that as a natural way to protect them from another pregnancy. Although it is true that breast-feeding will prevent ovulation for a certain amount of time, it's not forever and at most breast-feeding will delay ovulation only slightly. Also, because you'll have no warning that you've ovulated, relying on the fact that you're breast-feeding as a method of birth control is especially risky.

One point I made in the previous paragraph needs clarification, at least as it applies to certain women. *Mittelschmerz* is the pain that some women feel on ovulation. Women who have learned to recognize it can use this twinge of pain to help themselves plan a baby. Yet as for protecting themselves from an unintended pregnancy, that's another matter, because the woman might have had unprotected sex just before she felt that pain, and the sperm would survive long enough to fertilize the descending egg.

Abstinence

Certainly, abstinence can be a very effective method of birth control, but that's not to say that it's perfect. If a woman who has taken a vow of abstinence suddenly abandons that vow in the heat of passion, she will not be properly prepared and could end up having unprotected sex, and that could lead to an unintended pregnancy or worse. This happens far too often, so while abstinence is effective when it is being practiced, this drawback weakens its overall effectiveness. At the very least, someone who is practicing abstinence should become fully knowledgeable about the various means of contraception and should probably at least have some condoms on hand. Having condoms doesn't mean that you are going to use them, but they are there if needed.

Tubal Ligation

Tying and cutting the fallopian tubes could be considered the final option, because once these tubes have been interrupted, the woman should never be able to conceive a child.

For women, this is called a tubal ligation, and it involves cutting the fallopian tubes so that eggs cannot descend into the uterus and sperm cannot reach the eggs to fertilize them. It usually involves general anesthesia and minimal surgery, usually a laparoscopy, and is most often done in a hospital with the woman as an outpatient.

A tubal ligation procedure is considered permanent. It may be possible to reverse a tubal ligation, although in that case the surgery is more difficult and more costly (and not covered by health insurance).

Vasectomy

To render a man incapable of causing a pregnancy, the vas deferens, the tubes that deliver sperm to the other components of the ejaculate, are cut and tied off. The man continues to be able to ejaculate, but because there are no sperm, he cannot impregnate his partner. A vasectomy is a simpler and quicker procedure than female tubal ligation, and it is usually done under local anesthesia in a doctor's office and does not affect the man's ability to become sexually aroused. Also, because the amount of sperm within the ejaculate is small, the effect on the volume and quality of his ejaculate shouldn't be noticeable.

Although there are no guarantees that a vasectomy can be reversed, the procedure to reverse a vasectomy is much less complicated than trying to undo a tubal ligation, and the odds of success are much higher. A vasectomy is a very effective method of birth control, provided that the man waits the required three months during which he and his partner use another method of birth control. There can be sperm left over in his system from before the vasectomy that could cause a pregnancy before the full three months are up.

From Dr. Amos's Office: Erin and Robert's Story

A patient wanted to see me to talk about permanent birth control by tubal ligation. I asked that she come in with her husband. I explained the risks and benefits of tubal ligation for her and of a vasectomy for him. Because a vasectomy is much simpler and also because it is more easily reversed, I was able to convince them that the best course of action would be for him to get a vasectomy. He had the procedure done in a doctor's office, and they both were very happy about their decision.

Final Words

When it comes to avoiding an unintended pregnancy, my advice is to try to bring the risks as close to zero as possible. The consequences of a mistake happening are far too serious to adopt a relaxed attitude. Although no method of birth control is 100 percent effective, if you don't want to cause an unintended pregnancy, please make sure that you use at least one of the birth control methods mentioned in this chapter.

The Top Ten Forms of Birth Control

1. The pill
2. Condom
3. Depo-Provera
4. Tubal ligation
5. Vasectomy
6. IUD
7. Birth control patch
8. Natural family planning
9. Withdrawal
10. Abstinence

7

Planning for Pregnancy

In this chapter, you'll learn how to become pregnant. With so many women getting pregnant unintentionally, you might think it is the easiest thing in the world to do, yet for many couples it can be very difficult and sometimes even impossible. I'll cover every aspect of pregnancy, starting with what you should know before you become pregnant and including what you can do to become pregnant if you're having problems.

Getting Pregnant: Preconception Prep

First things first: folic acid.

Before you go on a road trip with your car, you make sure it's in good shape. You fill up the gas tank, check the tires, and see that there's enough oil. So, why do so many women get pregnant without preparing their bodies?

If pregnancy is in your future, whether it's next month or next year, the very first thing you should do is start taking folic acid, which is usually part of a prenatal vitamin supplement. Research has shown that if taken before conception (at least one to two months ahead of time), as well as during early pregnancy, folic acid can improve pregnancy outcome, which includes decreasing the risk of a miscarriage and preventing many birth defects. Every woman of childbearing age, even if she is not planning to become pregnant, should therefore supplement her diet with 400 to 600 micrograms of folic acid each day (ten times that amount or 4 mg if she or a family member has a history of neural tube defects, or NTDs).

It is important that this increased dosage be taken specifically from folic acid supplements in addition to eating a healthy diet. Taking prenatal vitamins in excess of the required dose is not recommended because of the potential risk of harm from high doses of the other vitamins. For folic acid to achieve its full effectiveness, you must start taking the supplement at least one to two months before conception.

A Preconception Visit to the Doctor

If you're planning to become pregnant, and after you have started taking your folic acid supplement, the next course of action should be a preconception visit with your Ob/Gyn. I understand that many couples who decide to try to have a baby want to keep it a secret. They don't want the added pressure of always having family and friends looking at them eagerly for news of whether a baby is on the way yet. But your relationship with your doctor is a totally private one, and a preconception visit could be vitally important to your health and that of your baby. So don't look at having this consultation as an announcement to the world that you're trying to have a baby, but rather take the attitude that it's an important first step to making the decision to having a child.

Here are a few examples of why this visit is so important. If you have a medical condition, such as diabetes, asthma, high blood pressure, or any other conditions for which you're taking medication, that medication could have a negative effect on your baby. Most medications are safe to take before and during pregnancy, but it's a good idea to confirm this with your doctor when you plan to get pregnant, and you should never stop taking medication on your own without consulting with a physician. If there's a need for you to cut back the dosage or take a different medication, your doctor will guide you through the steps to take. Of course, being pregnant will also affect other health conditions you may have, and you'll want to know what to expect and what to do about it.

Your doctor will need information on what over-the-counter medications you are taking, along with your use of tobacco, alcohol, and other drugs. Some studies have shown that even too much caffeine (usually, more than two cups a day of coffee, tea, or soda) can have a negative effect. If you need to stop certain habits, once you're pregnant is not the time to take action. You have to do it ahead of time. Your doctor can serve as an ally to help you.

You'll also be asked about your eating habits. Your overall diet is very important before as well as during pregnancy, and you'll appreciate the guidance that your doctor will give you. If you are planning on becoming pregnant, you should be following the same healthy diet as if you were pregnant. For example, fish should be part of your healthy balanced diet because it contains a lot of nutritious ingredients such as vitamin B, omega-3s, and protein. Yet there are some concerns about certain fish with high mercury levels, such as tilefish, swordfish, shark, and mackerel, which should not be eaten shortly before and during pregnancy. It's important to know which fish are safe and which are not and how much fish you can safely eat. You should also be careful with soft cheeses and undercooked meat, especially lamb, because these foods may increase your risk of developing a listeria or toxoplasma infection, which can increase complications during pregnancy.

Consult with your doctor about which foods to avoid, and, of course, you need to stop drinking alcohol while trying to conceive and during pregnancy. Your doctor may allow you an occasional glass of wine, but check first.

Vaccinations

Infections can be a problem even when you are not pregnant, but during pregnancy, you have two people to be concerned about. Vaccinations are available against several infections, and some vaccinations should not be given during your pregnancy. If you have any doubts about whether you've ever been vaccinated against certain childhood diseases, such as chicken pox, the time to get such a vaccination is before you get pregnant.

Lifestyle

There are also lifestyle issues to consider. For example, if you have cats, danger in the form of toxoplasmosis could lurk in the litter box, so you'll be advised to stay away from it. And because you never know what you might find in the garden, if you do any

---

From Dr. Amos's Office: Jennifer's Story

A patient saw me for a preconception visit and told me she wanted to get pregnant, but she was not immune to rubella, an infectious disease that could be very dangerous to the fetus if the mother became infected. I gave her a vaccine, and she was able to get pregnant soon after that, with the assurance that she was protected from this disease. Getting immunized for certain conditions prior to pregnancy will protect the mother and prevent the fetus from becoming affected.

gardening, you'll be told to always wear gloves and wash up carefully afterward.

Most couples who are thinking of having children are monogamous, but not all. Sometimes both partners are into having sex with other people, and other times only one partner does this, without the other one even knowing about it. The problem with this type of behavior is that it introduces an element of risk, in terms of possibly bringing a new sexually transmitted disease into the equation.

Your best course of action would be to stop this activity, but if for whatever reason you can't, then let your doctor know. Even if the man is cheating on his female partner, and he tells the doctor, the gynecologist will keep this news a secret. Yet at least the doctor will know to look for any signs of a sexually transmitted disease so that the baby is not at risk.

If you have any concerns about your genes and the possibility of passing on genetic propensities toward certain diseases, this would be the time to discuss the subject with your doctor. You could undergo tests that will determine the likelihood of whether your children might be in danger, and depending on the results, your doctor can advise you on how to handle such situations.

Finally, if you've already been pregnant, you'll want to discuss how this will affect your next pregnancy. In general, if you had no problems in a previous pregnancy, your next one will likely be uneventful as well, but if you did have a problem, there is a greater chance of it happening again. Depending on the type of birth you had, vaginal or cesarean section, you will be given various options to discuss with your doctor.

Although you may not need the advice of a doctor in the actual process of making a baby, talking to a doctor will give you added confidence that you are undertaking the creation of new life in the safest way possible.

Sex and Getting Pregnant

Despite the increase in technology to achieve pregnancies, such as in vitro fertilization (IVF) where the joining of the egg and the sperm happens outside the uterus in a dish, over 95 percent of pregnancies are achieved through good old-fashioned sex.

Many couples think they can just "do it" and get pregnant quickly. Nothing is further from the truth. Especially as a woman gets older, achieving pregnancy becomes more difficult. Many couples find out the hard way that it can take some time to get pregnant, and they are unaware of how they can improve their chances of getting pregnant.

First, you must know your fertile window. There are only five to six days of fertility during a woman's menstrual cycle: the day of ovulation and the five days before that day. You cannot get pregnant from making love more than five days before ovulation or from making love after ovulation. Research has shown that you are more likely to get pregnant if you make love once a day every day (or every other day, if he has a lower sperm count) during this five- to six-day fertile window. Making love more often than once a day likely decreases your chances of getting pregnant, and making love only once or twice during this period is not as effective as every day. Given this scenario, your first step in making a baby should be calculating the expected ovulation day.

Second, you must understand the mathematics of fertility. To find your fertile window, start by noting your first day of ovulation. Then take your average cycle length (usually between 21 and 35 days) and subtract 14. Add this number to the first day of your menstrual period. The first day of your cycle is the first day you bleed—the first day of your menstrual period. Here's an example: If your cycle is 30 days, then ovulation usually happens on cycle day 16 ($16 = 30 - 14$), which is the 16th day from the first day of your period (your menstrual bleeding). If you ovulate on cycle day 16, then you are most fertile that day, very fertile the two days before that day (cycle days 14 and 15), and slightly less fertile three days before that (cycle days 11, 12, and 13). In other words, you are potentially fertile between cycle days 11 and 16. Yet even with regular cycles, ovulation can happen on a different day. That's why, in addition to these five to six fertile days, you should also make love regularly two to three times a week every week of your entire cycle. There is no evidence that you can improve your chances of getting pregnant with an orgasm (he obviously has to have one to ejaculate), but it's clearly more fun.

If all this math is too much for you, go to an online fertility calendar (such as www.babymed.com/fertility-ovulation-calendar-calculator), enter your cycle length and date of last period, and the calculator will do the rest for you.

Many women have dry vaginas and often use lubricants during sex. This is okay when you're not trying to get pregnant, but when you are trying to get pregnant, lubricants won't help. In fact, most lubricants, including oils and water and even saliva, are known to kill sperm.

The most effective lubricant is the natural "self-made" human lubricant that is produced by a woman's vaginal glands. So try to make lubricant by prolonging foreplay, spending more time on pleasuring each other, and making sure the vagina is moist and ready before penetration. This will help the sperm move through the vagina into the uterus.

If you absolutely must use a lubricant and you are trying to conceive, you should find a lubricant that's specifically promoted as "sperm-friendly."

Fertility Issues

Just because you and a partner have made the decision to have a child doesn't mean that you'll immediately be successful. And just because you didn't have any problems getting pregnant in the past doesn't mean that you'll get pregnant quickly in subsequent attempts. About 50 percent of couples are successful within six months of beginning to try to get pregnant, but many factors can make it more difficult for you to become pregnant, including the stress that arises when you encounter difficulties. Couples who are stressed out are less likely to get pregnant, and one reason is that they don't make love often enough or don't make love during the fertile days.

If you've been trying to conceive for a while and not succeeding, usually more than twelve months for women under thirty-five and six months for women over thirty-five, then you should definitely make an appointment with your gynecologist. You should also see your doctor if you are beginning to try to get pregnant and you have medical or gynecological issues (having irregular menstrual periods is one condition that should make you see a doctor as soon as possible). Although some gynecologists specialize in infertility issues, most gynecologists can help you initially determine the nature of the problem, which might come from an unexpected source.

From Dr. Amos's Office: Hannah's Story

An orthodox Jewish woman came to see me because for the last year she'd been trying to have a baby and couldn't seem to get pregnant. When assessing a woman's fertility, among the important factors for a gynecologist to determine is whether she is ovulating. I call ovulation the "Big O" (and that's different from the Big O in Dr. Ruth's field, which is orgasm). The length and regularity of the menstrual cycle, the time between the first day of the last period and the first day of the next period, can give a hint of her ability to ovulate. No menstrual bleeding or very irregular bleeding usually indicates that there is a problem with ovulation. Although the average menstrual cycle length is defined as taking place during a 28-day period, many women have cycles that are shorter or longer than the normal range, somewhere between 21 and

35 days. It turned out that this Jewish woman had regular menstrual cycles of 22 days. She had her menstrual period every 22 days for 4 days. If ovulation takes place, the next period usually begins 14 days after ovulation, so in a 22-day cycle, ovulation would happen on cycle day 8 (menstrual cycle length minus 14 = 22 minus 14 = 8). Yet according to Jewish law, she wasn't allowed to have sex until 7 days after the end of her menstrual period or bleeding, which in her case was around cycle day 11. Fertilization cannot happen if you make love after ovulation, however, and if she made love on cycle day 11, then she missed her ovulation by 3 days and could not get pregnant. As long as she was going to follow the strictures of her religion, she would not be able to become pregnant.

The solution turned out to be an easy one. I first checked out her husband, who turned out to be fertile, and I then gave her medication that delayed ovulation so that she began ovulating at the time when she was permitted to have intercourse. Two months after starting this treatment, she became pregnant. By the way, she had twins, which is not so unusual when taking this medication.

As you should know, problems with conceiving could stem from the man or the woman (or sometimes both). In fact, about one in two cases of infertility has a "male cause." Because testing the man's sperm is the easiest, and especially if the woman's ovulation cycle is regular, examining his sperm should be among the first steps in assessing a couple's fertility. His ejaculate will be tested for overall volume and concentration of sperm. At least 40 million sperm are necessary for him to be considered fertile (even though only one of those 40 million will succeed). This doesn't mean that a man who produces fewer sperm can't cause a pregnancy, but it lowers the odds significantly and at the very least means that it will take longer. In addition to counting the number of sperm and the volume of the ejaculate, the spermanalysis also determines whether they are viable, are good swimmers (motility), and have normal shapes (morphology).

From Dr. Amos's Office: Juliet and Mark's Story

A couple came to see me who were having problems conceiving. Her cycle was normal, so I had his sperm tested, and it turned out that his sperm count was low, with only a million viable sperm per ejaculation. In having him checked out, I discovered that he had a variococele, an enlargement of the veins in the testes, which leads to increased temperature. The reason that a man's testicles hang outside his body is that too much heat lowers his sperm count. With this condition (the variococele), the increased heat rendered the man infertile. Only minor surgery was required to fix the problem, and three months later his wife became pregnant.

I recommend that the spermanalysis be the very first fertility test, and what better test could there be than one that requires the person getting tested to have an orgasm?

If everything is normal with your partner's sperm, then you'll be checked out next. When a couple has difficulty getting pregnant and the man has a normal spermanalysis, there can be several causes for a woman's difficulties to conceive. It could have to do with her ovaries and ovulation; a condition called PCOS (polycystic ovarian syndrome) is the number one reason for younger women to have ovulation and fertility issues. Or it could be the quality of her eggs, a condition that often happens as a woman gets older but can also happen in younger women. Blood tests can quickly determine the quality of a woman's eggs.

Or else something could be wrong with the delivery system, such as a blockage in the fallopian tubes. Or perhaps the problem has to do with the fertilized egg or embryo not attaching itself to the womb.

Determining the cause of most fertility problems is not so difficult and can often be done in one to two months. Then finding a solution will become more likely. There are, however, about 15 to 20 percent of couples with "unexplained infertility," which means that all tests are normal, and they still cannot get pregnant. In those cases, infertility specialists usually suggest in vitro fertilization to improve the couple's chances having a baby.

Following is a periconception check-off list that will help you improve your pregnancy outcome even before you are pregnant:

Three Months Prior to Conception

- Begin periconceptional multivitamin supplementation, especially with folic acid.
- Find a good obstetrician or a maternal-fetal medicine (MFM) specialist now (do not wait until your pregnancy is confirmed).
- Get examined and take the following tests:
  - Sperm analysis to check his fertility.
  - Vaginal and cervical smear examination to screen for sexually transmitted infections/disorders.
  - Blood tests for rubella, anemia, HIV, and genetic screening of autosomal and X-linked recessive carrier status and recently for predictive gene diagnostic tests. Determine prior exposure to toxoplasma, cytomegalovirus, parvovirus, and herpes.
  - Any additional tests, if necessary.
- Get immunized for rubella, if not immune, and other conditions, if indicated.
- Begin to follow a healthy diet and engage in moderate exercise (both you and your partner).
- Switch any less safe medications to safer ones. Your partner should stay away from any potential hazards and keep his testes "cool."
- Give the doctor your occupational history so that he or she can check for occupational hazards.
- Try to reach an optimal BMI if you're overweight.

During the Three Months Leading Up to Conception

- Avoid active or passive smoking, drink no alcohol, and don't take any unnecessary drugs. Limit coffee to one to two cups a day.

- Follow your menstrual cycle, and consider measuring your basal body temperatures to detect hormonal dysfunction (and undergo treatment, if necessary) and determine the optimal day to make love and achieve conception (two to three days prior to, plus on the day of, ovulation).
- Continue periconception multivitamin supplementation.
- See a dentist and check your dental status.
- Continue doing moderate physical exercise.

Early Pregnancy

- Early pregnancy confirmation, if necessary, blood hCG measurements (a urine pregnancy test is usually positive around the time of a missed period, the blood test is usually positive three to four days earlier).
- Call your doctor as soon as you are pregnant for any further examinations and/or treatments.
- Begin postconceptional multivitamin supplementation.
- Avoid any risks that may harm the fetus (no alcohol, no smoking or other potentially harmful drugs).
- Undergo an early ultrasound to evaluate the pregnancy around six to eight weeks.

The Impact on Your Sex Life

One major difficulty that couples with fertility issues encounter is the impact it has on their sex lives. Before their infertility became a problem, sex was likely a fun and pleasurable experience that each partner shared; it was part of the glue that kept their relationship healthy. Yet once fertility issues arise, the nature of their sexual relationship changes. First of all, every time they have sex now, they are reminded of their inability to make a baby. That can put a damper on one or both partners' desire for sex. If the quality of their sex life takes a turn for the worse, they may develop relationship problems. The overall stress then can have a negative impact on the woman's ability to conceive, so that it becomes a vicious cycle.

It's also possible that having sex ends up being put on a time-table. The idea is to make sure that you have sex on days when you are likely to be fertile. This means you'll closely monitor your body so that you'll know the time is right. Yet it also means that your partner has to be ready with as much sperm as possible, so he shouldn't have any orgasms for a few days prior to your fertile period. If people have to obey a timetable that dictates when they can have sex, it can turn into a chore, instead of a joy. Although it's not necessary for sex to always be spontaneous, it certainly detracts from the excitement if it's never a spur-of-the-moment decision and always a scheduled event.

By the way, even couples who have just started trying and haven't run into any difficulties yet can encounter these problems to a lesser degree. If you're thinking about whether "this time" might make you pregnant, then such thoughts could overwhelm your ability to become aroused. And if you're having intercourse but not fully enjoying it, that is, not having orgasms, you could potentially create a pattern that would have an impact after you've had the baby. If you become too fixated on the baby-making aspects of sex and forget that sex is also an expression of love between you and your partner, this could drive a wedge between the two of you. It may be hard to think twenty-five years or so into the future, but eventu-ally your baby will move on to form his or her own life and you and your partner will remain together. So never forget that you have to continue to nurture this adult relationship, even as you're attaching yourself to a baby, which may not even be a fertilized egg yet.

The key to keeping your sex life healthy while you're trying to conceive, whether or not you're having difficulties, is to maintain good communication. It's true that you can't prevent certain feelings from welling up, such as feeling sad during sex if you've been trying to have a child for a long time, but how you handle this will play an important role on the effect it has on your relationship. For example, if you try to put up a false front and pretend that you're not sad but then don't get any enjoyment out of having sex, that's only going to exacerbate the situation, in both the short run and the long run. But if you tell your partner that you feel sad, and he comforts you, then hopefully you can get back in the mood, and your level of arousal will rise, and you'll actually enjoy having sex. That will help maintain your relationship.

You may also want to discuss this outside of the bedroom. The best location might be on a walk down a quiet country road, where you'll have plenty of privacy, but it could be anywhere, just not in the room where you normally have sex. You want to keep that place free from memories of anything negative, to the degree that you possibly can. Obviously, if you're trying to have sex, and it's not working, and you start crying, you don't need to rush out of the room. But if you agree to have a planned discussion about your sex life, make sure to do it somewhere other than your bedroom.

You might also consider having sex in other parts of the house besides the bedroom. Maybe you could do it at times when you know you're not likely to be fertile so that you create two sex lives, which may help your overall desire for sex. Or you could simply add a lot of variety to your sex life in all sorts of ways during the time you're trying to make a baby, so that you don't fall into a rut that will constantly remind you of any failures.

The Financial Impact

Although the most basic modalities of treatment for infertility are simple and don't require much of an investment, monetarily speaking, such as measuring your body's temperature in order to find out if and when you ovulate and are most fertile, other treatments can be very expensive and are rarely covered by insurance. Some people say they will spare no expense in order to have a child, while many others have no choice but to place a limit on what they can spend.

It's a good idea for you and your partner to discuss this issue before you even talk to a doctor. It's easy for a misunderstanding to arise, so that one partner thinks that you're both going to spend whatever it takes, while the other isn't willing to spend more than a certain amount. When the two of you have set a budget, you need to bring up this topic with the doctor. You can't expect your doctor to know what your financial commitment is going to be, but his or her advice may be different, depending on that information. People need to consider many factors when making decisions about fertility treatment, including the age of the mother, for example, but often financial considerations are among the most important.

When the Problem Lies within You

If your partner's sperm are fine, then the difficulties you are experiencing in getting pregnant probably lie somewhere within you. Unless your gynecologist happens to be an expert in fertility issues, you'll probably have to consult another doctor. These days, solving fertility problems has become very high-tech, which

---

From Dr. Amos's Office: Amanda's Story

A woman came to see me saying that she'd been trying for several years to become pregnant but hadn't had any success. She was about 5 foot 3 inches and weighed 195 pounds. A quick calculation to assess her body mass index (BMI) (see the table that follows) showed that her BMI was 34.5, which is considered obese. A normal BMI is between 18.5 and 24.9. A BMI below 18.5 is underweight, and a BMI above 24.9 is overweight. A BMI of 30 and greater is considered obese. One common side effect of being overweight for women is an irregular cycle, usually due to ovulation problems. I determined that her cycle was somewhere between forty-five and sixty days, which meant that the odds of her ovulating normally and getting pregnant were significantly reduced. I put her on a diet-and-exercise program, and in a six-month-period, she lost 46 pounds, and her BMI went down to 26.4. That weight loss helped her ovulate and regularized her monthly cycle, and three months after that, she became pregnant.

| Body Mass Index | | | | | | | | | | | | | |
Weight (lbs)	100	110	120	130	140	150	160	170	180	190	200	210	220	230
Height (ft/in)														
5'0"	20	21	23	25	27	29	31	33	35	37	39	41	43	45
5'1"	19	21	23	25	26	28	30	32	34	36	38	40	42	43
5'2"	18	20	22	24	26	27	29	31	33	35	37	38	40	42
5'3"	18	19	21	23	25	27	28	30	32	34	35	37	39	41
5'4"	17	19	21	22	24	26	27	29	31	33	34	36	38	39
5'5"	17	18	20	22	23	25	27	28	30	32	33	35	37	38
5'6"	16	18	19	21	23	24	26	27	29	31	32	34	36	37
5'7"	16	17	19	20	22	23	25	27	28	30	31	33	34	36
5'8"	15	17	18	20	21	23	24	26	27	29	30	32	33	35
5'9"	15	16	18	19	21	22	24	25	27	28	30	31	32	34
5'10"	14	16	17	19	20	22	23	24	26	27	29	30	32	33
5'11"	14	15	17	18	20	21	22	24	25	26	28	29	31	32
6'0"	14	15	16	18	19	20	22	23	24	26	27	28	30	31
6'1"	13	15	16	17	18	20	21	22	24	25	26	28	29	30
6'2"	13	14	15	17	18	19	21	22	23	24	26	27	28	30
6'3"	12	14	15	16	17	19	20	21	22	24	25	26	27	29
6'4"	12	13	15	16	17	18	19	21	22	23	24	26	27	28

Find your weight (round up to the nearest number) on the horizontal axis and your height on the vertical axis. The intersection of those two numbers is your BMI. A normal BMI is considered to be between 18.5 and 24.9.

means the odds that you'll be helped have increased greatly. That doesn't mean it's going to be easy or inexpensive, but knowing that success is much more likely today than ever before will give you great comfort.

It's common knowledge that obesity can lead to diabetes and high blood pressure, but it's much less well known that obese women not only have a more difficult time becoming pregnant but are more prone to having miscarriages and developing other complications during pregnancy, such as premature births, cesarean section, and other medical problems. If you are overweight or obese, your first step should be to work at losing weight. This is true for everyone, not only those with fertility issues. And if you think being overweight is only a problem for the woman, then you should think again. Being overweight also decreases a man's fertility, and losing weight could improve his chances of making you pregnant.

Because fertility issues are so complex, I'd need an entire book to explain everything in detail. Since I don't have room for that, I'm going to give you a simple overview. Whether you'd like to learn more at some point or simply rely on your doctor's expertise will be up to you. Just remember that stress plays a role in whether you succeed, and if knowing too much and becoming too involved in the nitty-gritty details of the process will make you more stressed, then perhaps the better approach is to find a doctor you trust and put yourself in his or her hands. If your partner is the type who wants to learn as much as possible, don't stop him. But if you don't feel like delving into all of the technical details because it will only drive you crazy, then tell him that you'd prefer not to have deep discussions on this subject.

Tests

A fertility specialist (reproductive endocrinologist, or RE) will usually do some blood work on you to test certain hormone levels that influence your ability to become pregnant, such as, during the first days of your cycle, follicle-stimulating hormone (FSH), luteinizing hormone (LH), thyroid-stimulating hormone (TSH), estrogens, prolactin, and possibly androgens. About a week after that, he or she will also test for ovulation progesterone hormone.

Doing a basal body temperature curve may help identify if and when you ovulate. You'll be told to take your oral or rectal temperature first thing in the morning, before you get out of bed. By keeping a record, after a month or two, you should see when it goes up slightly, indicating if and when your ovaries have released an egg. This may be important in order to determine whether you made love at the right time (remember, there are five to six fertile days, the day of ovulation and the five to six days before that day).

Assuming that your hormone levels are within a certain range, you are ovulating regularly, and your partner's sperm count is fine, the next tests that many doctors order are a hysterosalpingogram and maybe a laparoscopy. A hysterosalpingogram is either an X-ray or a sonogram, during which dye or saline is injected through the cervix to see whether your fallopian tubes are open. A laparoscopy means that your doctor will place a camera through your abdomen to have a careful look at your uterus. You will have to be put under general anesthesia for this test, but it will be done on an outpatient basis, meaning that you won't have to stay overnight in the hospital.

During these tests, your doctor will want to make sure that your fallopian tubes aren't blocked and that you don't have any fibroids, cysts, endometriosis (lining of the uterus outside the uterus), or scar tissue that might be preventing a fertilized egg from moving normally through the fallopian tubes. If it turns out that you do have a problem of this nature, then surgery or other treatments, such as in vitro fertilization, may be recommended.

If ovulation is the problem, and your tubes are normal and his sperm count is normal, then many doctors recommend certain drugs to induce your ovaries to mature more eggs and make you ovulate. If you decide that this is the approach you will take, your doctor will bring you in several times to do blood tests to determine which would be the best day to administer these drugs.

There are several different drugs, as well as different methods of administering them. Taking a drug in pill form is usually first recommended. Which drug will depend on a variety of factors, including cost and side effects. This is not always an easy decision and is one that you must go over carefully with your doctor.

If the pills are not effective, then hormonal shots would be the next method to induce ovulation to help you get pregnant. Your doctor will explain that these shots are likely to have more side effects, such as bloating, and that your chances of having multiple births will also increase.

Basically, what in vitro fertilization (IVF) means is that eggs are surgically removed from the female, mixed with the male's sperm outside the body, where they hopefully will become fertilized, and then replaced into the female's womb. Several eggs are replaced in the hopes that at least one will become fertilized. If you and your partner have fertilization issues so that his sperm can't be used, the sperm of another man may be substituted. In addition to IVF, doctors also use a procedure called intracytoplasmic sperm injection (ICSI) to improve your chances of getting pregnant. During ICSI a single sperm is injected with a tiny needle directly into the egg. It is mostly used when there is a male infertility problem.

IVF involves more than the procedures described previously. Once the eggs are implanted, you will have to go for daily blood tests and will get hormone injections, some of which are quite painful. In addition, there may be minor side effects, such as bloating and nausea, and even more serious side effects, such as damage to the liver and the kidneys.

Whether IVF will be successful depends to some degree on your age and the reason for the infertility. In younger women, usually one out of three women becomes pregnant after IVF, but those odds increase the older a woman (and her eggs) get. The likelihood of having twins, assuming you do get pregnant, is high, especially if more than one fertilized egg is implanted. Twins are associated with many more pregnancy complications, including more miscarriages and premature deliveries, longer stays in the neonatal intensive care units, and long-term developmental issues. The chance of having two or more babies usually depends on how many embryos are implanted. The more embryos that are implanted, the higher your risk of having twins, triplets, or more. Before undergoing fertility treatments and especially IVF, you should discuss with your doctor how to decrease your risk of having multiple births and, especially with IVF, whether one or more embryos should be implanted. Research has shown that transferring only one embryo can have as high a pregnancy success rate as implanting more, and transferring one embryo can significantly decrease your chances of having twins. Of course, it might not work at all, and then you'd be faced with the decision of whether to go through the process again.

Miscarriages

So far, I've reviewed what could go wrong if your eggs aren't getting fertilized, but a whole series of other problems can arise after fertilization, so that the egg doesn't implant in the womb and instead gets flushed out. The term for this is either *spontaneous abortion* or *miscarriage.*

A miscarriage is the loss of a pregnancy before twenty weeks. In general, there is a 30 to 40 percent chance of having a miscarriage. The older you are, the more likely you are to have a miscarriage. Women younger than thirty-five have a 15 to 20 percent chance of having a miscarriage, but that percentage increases quickly, and a woman older than forty has a 40 to 50 percent or higher chance of miscarriage.

The main reason miscarriages occur is that something is genetically wrong with the embryo, the fertilized egg, so even if it properly implants, it may not develop. If you've had several miscarriages (and it's possible that you might not know that you've had an early miscarriage) or if your doctor suspects that you may have been having them, he or she will perform certain tests, which may include checking both partners' chromosomes and doing various blood tests. You may also undergo an endometrial biopsy, which means that some tissue from the walls of your uterus will be scraped off for analysis. The results of such tests will give the doctor clues about how to prevent you from having any more miscarriages, if the problem has something to do with fertilized eggs not implanting themselves in your uterus.

How do you know whether you've had a miscarriage? Many miscarriages happen before a woman realizes that she is pregnant. Her period may be slightly delayed or heavier than usual. Unless you have had a positive pregnancy test, you won't know. Other miscarriages are associated with some lower back pain, similar to or worse than menstrual cramps, and you might feel actual cramping as if in labor. There may be some light bleeding; however, be aware that up to a third of pregnant women experience some light bleeding during the first three to four months of pregnancy, and of those, most go on to have a normal delivery. (These symptoms could actually be a result of the fertilized egg being implanted in the wall of the uterus or other issues.) You might even notice that some actual tissue material is expelled from your vagina. Other signs of pregnancy, such as swollen breasts, will disappear.

Sometimes a woman can experience a miscarriage and not see any visible signs: no bleeding, no loss of tissue, and no cramping. (In fact, she may not have known that she was pregnant in the first place.) In most cases, the miscarriage happens early in the pregnancy, and the buildup of tissue is minimal and gets completely expelled. The later in pregnancy that a miscarriage occurs, the more tissue is involved and the greater the chance that all of the material will not be expelled. Because this can lead to infection or more bleeding, a surgical procedure, known as a D&C (dilation and curettage), is performed, which means the doctor must scrape out the lining of the uterus to make sure that nothing of the pregnancy remains.

Assuming that you were trying to have a baby, all miscarriages are sad events, although the latter type can be the most emotionally trying, because it involves a procedure that is similar to an abortion. This is not a time when you have to keep a stiff upper lip. It's all right to feel very sad and to mourn the loss of this opportunity to have a baby. You don't want to dwell on what happened, but you should allow yourself to experience the feelings of sadness so that you can get over them quickly and go back to trying to become pregnant again with as much positive energy as possible.

Although in most cases, there is nothing that you can do to avoid a miscarriage (after all, you can't control the genetic material that went into making a particular embryo), to minimize the chances of having another miscarriage and to safeguard the health of any future live births, you should definitely make sure that you take very good care of your body. Taking folic acid supplements well before you become pregnant could improve the pregnancy outcome. You should watch what you eat and get as much exercise as your doctor allows. Do not smoke and stay away from cigarette smoke altogether. You shouldn't drink any alcohol and should limit your intake of caffeine. If your workplace contains any environmental hazards, speak to your employer about allowing you to move to a location that limits your contact with such hazards as much as possible and perhaps eliminates your exposure altogether.

At the other extreme of a miscarriage is an ectopic pregnancy, which occurs when the embryo implants itself someplace other than the uterus, most commonly in one of the fallopian tubes, and begins to develop. This can be life threatening to the mother and requires surgery as soon as it is detected.

From Dr. Amos's Office: Jane's Story

Jane was a twenty-eight-year-old woman who previously had surgery on one of her fallopian tubes. She had missed her period and used an over-the-counter pregnancy test, which told her she was pregnant. A week later, she discovered that she was spotting, that is, she found spots of blood in her panties, and she developed a dull pain in her lower right side. When she came to see me, her last period had been about six weeks earlier. While I performed my examination, she reported some pain when I touched her cervix. I did a sonogram in my office to see whether anything could be detected in her uterus, but although she was apparently pregnant, there was nothing inside the uterus. A blood test showed that her blood hCG pregnancy hormone level was 2,300 mIU/ml, and in a repeat test forty-eight hours later, it rose less than 15 percent to only 2,700 mIU/ml (I normally expect the hCG level to go up at this point of the pregnancy by at least *50 to 60* percent). At that level, I would have expected to see a pregnancy inside her uterus, and this information, together with her prior history and the slower-than-expected rise in hCG, made me suspect that she had an ectopic pregnancy. She was medically stable, so I treated her with an intramuscular injection of a medication called methotrexate, which stops the growth of the embryo.

The following week, her pregnancy hCG hormone levels had dropped significantly, and she felt better. Seven weeks later, her pregnancy test was negative.

When a woman has one ectopic pregnancy, it's likely that she'll have another, which is why it is very important for such women to go to see their gynecologists as soon as they suspect that they are pregnant. If the doctor detects an ectopic pregnancy early enough, it may be possible to save the other fallopian tube. If it's too late, and the embryo has grown too big or the tube has ruptured, then that tube will often have to be removed, and she will not be able to conceive a child naturally.

I can't let this chapter end on such a sad note. I don't want to be a Pollyanna and pretend that all of these issues can simply be cast aside, but I want to emphasize here that no matter what the outcome, you and your partner must protect your relationship so that you can be a strong support for each other. Having a baby is wonderful, but a loving relationship is also very valuable, and you must make sure that you hold on to it, whatever the outcome of your quest to have children.

The Top Ten Preconception Steps

1. Start taking folic acid supplements and a daily multivitamin.
2. Have a preconception doctor's visit.
3. Have all necessary vaccinations.

4. Stop drinking alcohol.

5. Stop your tobacco intake.

6. Limit your coffee intake.

7. Eat healthy food.

8. Keep away from cat litter.

9. Begin an exercise program.

10. Make love once a day during your fertile days and regularly throughout your cycle.

8

A Healthy Pregnancy

In this chapter, you'll learn what happens during each trimester when you are pregnant. This includes information that I feel is crucial: when you can have sex and when you can't.

For millennia, women had their babies without the help of doctors. They birthed them out in the fields or in their caves or wherever, perhaps with the help of other women and perhaps not. In some places in the world, that's still the way it happens. So why does a woman need an obstetrician when she discovers she's pregnant? The biggest reason is that so many of those women who went into labor without the benefits of modern medicine died in the process, as did their children. Although giving birth is the most natural of occurrences, it also carries a lot of risks.

Assuming that you're not going to chance giving birth without medical supervision, what do you need to know? I will go over some of the basics, but there are dozens of books devoted to just this subject, where you can find a lot more detail than I have room for here. What I'm going to concentrate on in this chapter are two areas that are not covered in depth in most books on pregnancy—sex during pregnancy and how to make best use of your Ob/Gyn.

Your Due Date

The due date is among the most important pieces of information to be determined during pregnancy. Everything in pregnancy revolves around the due date. Every woman wants her obstetrician to tell her the date her baby will be born, even though only 5 percent of babies are born on their due date; most are born within two weeks before or after their due date. For a doctor to accurately answer that question, he or she would have to know the exact day you became pregnant, and often there may be no precise answer to that question, which in turn is why there are many different ways of timing your pregnancy.

Knowing the first day of the last menstrual period is usually the first step in determining the due date. if you're trying to get pregnant and want to know your due date to the greatest degree of accuracy, I suggest that you keep a diary of your menstrual periods and the days you had unprotected intercourse (if you also keep track of your basal body temperature, that will help increase the accuracy of the prediction). Yes, offering these statistics to your doctor might be a little embarrassing, but that type of information is very useful in coming up with a due date.

The method that doctors use most frequently to calculate your due date is called the gestational age method, and it is measured by adding 280 days from the first day of your last period. A more accurate method would be to add 266 days from the day of ovulation or fertilization, if you know that day. With this method, pregnancy is determined in weeks and days from the first day of your last period. This can sometimes be confusing, because when your gestational age is, for example, fourteen weeks, you are in fact only twelve weeks pregnant, because in most cases fertilization and ovulation happen around two weeks after the first day of your menstrual period. The fetal age is the actual age of the growing fetus from the time of conception, but, as I said, that may not be known unless you're aware of exactly when you ovulated, you had a basal body temperature curve or took drugs to induce ovulation, or you had in vitro fertilization. So while a pregnancy is supposed to last nine months (or, more precisely, your due date is supposed to occur 266 days from ovulation/fertilization or 280 days from your last period), calculating your due date is far from an exact science, both because your doctor often simply estimates the exact date you became pregnant and because your body may decide to go into labor either earlier or later than what is considered average.

Other ways to determine how far along you are in your pregnancy are by having sonograms done and by measuring the fetus. The earlier in pregnancy that a sonogram is done, the more precise it is in determining the due date, which is another reason that you need to see a doctor as soon as you know you are pregnant, assuming you haven't gone beforehand as I suggested.

The Trimester System

Pregnancy is usually divided into three trimesters, based on the development of the fetus and the changes that you will undergo, although, for your growing baby, development occurs every day, and these trimesters actually have little meaning other than as an indication of how you may feel.

Your first trimester begins at the time of conception, when a sperm enters an egg you've released. This usually occurs in the fallopian tubes, and it takes from six to twelve days for the fertilized egg to make its way down into the uterus and implant itself into the uterine lining. Until that happens, your body has no idea that pregnancy has begun, but once implantation occurs, you will often begin to notice some changes within days, especially if you are attuned to them. These changes are caused by the increase in your hCG pregnancy hormone levels. Your breasts might swell a bit and feel tender. You might also see a difference in the coloration of the areolas. You might feel nauseous, especially in the morning, and have some unexpected bleeding, which will occur as a direct result of implantation. Don't be surprised if you feel more tired and if the time between trips to the bathroom grows a lot shorter. While you're experiencing these symptoms, your baby is making quite a lot of progress as well. In fact, by seven weeks into your pregnancy, it's possible to pick up a tiny heartbeat with a sonogram.

Most women find that they've never felt better than during their second trimester. You'll be wearing maternity clothes, because your belly will have made your old wardrobe obsolete, but that means your baby has grown a lot and is getting ready to greet the world. In fact, it's during the second semester, usually around the fourteen-week mark, that the quickening occurs. This means that you'll be able to feel your baby move around. What a great feeling that is!

On the down side, you may start to see stretch marks on your belly and may notice some skin discoloration, even on your face, which is sometimes called the mask of pregnancy. Itchy skin on your abdomen, your palms, and the soles of your feet may be annoying, but if the itching is accompanied by a sudden, extreme weight gain, nausea, and jaundice, let your doctor know as soon as possible, because these symptoms could be signs of a liver problem. You may also notice swelling of your ankles, fingers, and face. If that swelling becomes extreme, and you also gain a lot of weight suddenly, go see your doctor immediately because those could be signs of preeclampsia, which is a dangerous condition.

Communicating with Your Doctor

Your third trimester is when you really begin to feel as if you're going to have a baby. You'll want to be reading those books you bought so that you can get the answers to the flood of questions that you'll have, especially about how labor will be for you. Those books, if you've selected the right ones, can give you more information than you can digest, and because you know your doctor is a busy

---

From Dr. Amos's Office: The Importance of Communication

I've lost count of how many babies I've delivered. Hearing that patient X or Y has gone into labor doesn't cause me to panic; it's just part of my normal workday. But for my patients, it's very important that they have full confidence in me because the more confident they are, the better the outcome of labor will be for them. Sometimes they have to push very hard to avoid having a C-section. They have to believe me when I tell them that they can do it. They mustn't think that I don't really care, that I'm only some stranger with medical knowledge. That's why the communications that I have with my patients during the entire course of their pregnancies are so important. The closeness of our relationship will really come into play in the delivery room, but it's not something that can happen instantly. It's a relationship that needs to form over time. That's why it's important that you ask your doctor questions. It's not what he or she tells you, it's the fact that you're communicating and building a relationship, so that when the time comes for you to give birth, the two of you will work together as a team, confident in each other's abilities.

---

person, you might think that you shouldn't bother him or her with all of your questions. (Of course, some women have the reverse problem and bombard their doctor with questions that they could easily get the answers to elsewhere.) But what I want to point out here is that talking to your doctor at this point isn't so much about transferring information as it is about team building.

Sex during Pregnancy

Although engaging in sex is what causes pregnancy, the issue of whether a couple can continue to have sex during pregnancy is often a stumbling block. While the answer to the basic question of whether it's okay to have sex is yes, it's not always as simple as that.

Assuming this is your first baby, it's important even during pregnancy that this child doesn't have a serious, long-term negative impact on your sex life with your partner. The key word is *long-term*. If a couple doesn't have sex for a short period of time because of pregnancy and postpartum issues, that shouldn't have an effect on their overall relationship. Yet sometimes other issues can develop during this nonsexual time period that can have long-lasting and damaging repercussions. Some new moms become so engrossed with and exhausted by motherhood that they lose their desire for sex, and the couple's sex life can become permanently damaged. Some new dads suddenly see their wives more as mothers than as sexual beings, and they may have difficulties becoming aroused by their wives. A sexless marriage is one that is in great danger, so you have to overcome these obstacles, rather than ignore them. I'll get into more detail in a bit.

The basic answer to whether it's safe to engage in intercourse is that the penis entering the vagina cannot harm the child unless there is some sort of medical complication. Some women are more likely to have a premature birth if they have sex. Also, if you have a condition called placenta previa, your doctor will forbid you from having intercourse. But for most couples, other than making adjustments for the woman's growing belly, which will render some positions impossible during the third trimester, intercourse poses no danger to the child.

From Dr. Amos's Office: Restrictions on Sex

Examples of when your doctor may suggest that you do not make love during pregnancy include

If you are at risk of having a premature birth or labor.

If you are having multiples (twins, triplets).

If you have a weak or short cervix.

If you have placenta previa (where part of the placenta is covering the cervix).

If your water has broken.

If you experience vaginal bleeding.

If you or your partner has an active sexually transmitted disease.

You may have noticed that I've been using the word *intercourse*. A couple can still give each other sexual satisfaction even if intercourse is off limits. I would strongly suggest that the woman continue to play a role in her partner's sex life, even if she doesn't feel like having orgasms herself. What happens if she doesn't? The man will feel sexually frustrated, so he'll masturbate. In most cases, that's not a big deal. Many people with partners masturbate when they feel the desire for sexual release and their partners don't. Yet what's different about this situation is that the period of time when the couple's normal love life is interrupted could last for months. Reestablishing normal relations after such a long time could be problematic. Maybe the man has felt free to use porn during this time and finds that he doesn't want to give it up so easily. If the woman needs a kick-start to get her sexual desire going again, and he's not that eager to help because he's found other outlets, their sex life could wind up seriously damaged.

To most men, the whole process of pregnancy is a bit mysterious, so they give a lot of leeway to their pregnant partners. They're a little afraid that if something goes wrong, they'll get blamed, so they're willing to go out of their way to please their wives. When it comes to little things, such as getting ice cream at midnight, that's more a sign for the woman that her partner is there for her than it is a need for ice cream. It's a confidence builder more than anything else. Yet sex is also a confidence builder. It tells the woman that her partner still finds her attractive, and it tells the man the same thing. When sex is taken out of the equation, it reduces both of their confidence levels. It's natural to feel a little nervous when your family is about to undergo such a drastic change, and maintaining your sexual relationship is an important bond.

So, what am I suggesting? First, that you not put sex on the back burner. Even if you can't have intercourse, maintain as much of your sexual relationship as possible. Don't just give each other a peck on the cheek but really kiss. Touch each other's bodies sensually. Give each other orgasms, no matter what method you use. Continue to be sexual partners, as well as new parents. Make sex a priority, and you, your relationship, and therefore even your child will benefit.

If you have any questions, ask your doctor. Even if your doctor says you shouldn't do X, Y, or Z, you'll also know that you can do A, B, and C. Having the confidence that certain sexual activities are entirely safe will make it more likely that you engage in sexual activity. But if you're in the dark and secretly worried that having sex might endanger your pregnancy in some way, then you'll avoid all sexual activity. For example, you won't kiss sensually because you'll be afraid of producing feelings of arousal. So although you absolutely need to carefully nurture that new baby growing inside of you, at the same time you also have to nurture and pay attention to your sex life.

Your twenty-ninth week of pregnancy announces the beginning of your third trimester, and the finish line is almost in sight. With your baby having grown so much, many of your organs are being squeezed, which will undoubtedly cause you to feel the urge to urinate more often, may give you constipation, and could even make breathing more difficult. By the beginning of your third trimester, you should have begun any childbirth classes you and your partner were planning to take, just in case you don't make it all of the way, which can be the result of faulty calculations or a baby who is impatient and can't wait for the full term to be up. As you near the end of the road, you'll be visiting your doctor more often because you'll both want to see how you're progressing.

Your uterus will have to put on quite a show to force the baby out. In order for it to have the necessary strength, it's going to practice from time to time. These practice contractions you may feel are called Braxton-Hicks. They are harmless, unless they happen before thirty-seven weeks. If you do feel regular contractions before thirty-seven weeks, you should contact your doctor or go to the hospital to make sure you are not in premature labor.

With Braxton-Hicks contractions, at first you may think that you're going into labor, but although this will be the first time you feel these sensations and they will feel odd, these practice contractions are not strong enough and regular enough and do not last long enough to cause your baby to come out.

As I said earlier, having sex while pregnant poses no dangers to the baby. Of course, you'll be a lot less comfortable, and you may lose your desire for sex because of that. In some cases, your partner will lose his desire, mostly out of fear that he could endanger the baby. As in the second semester, if you both feel like having sex, know that you can safely have sex, including orgasms; you simply have to find comfortable positions. Although I never want any couple to have sex under pressure, as I've stated, it's important not to allow your sex life to die out altogether, so don't take what may appear to be the easy way out and avoid sex.

As the time approaches for you to have your baby, you'll discover that your doctor is most concerned about how dilated your cervix is. No matter how strongly you feel the practice contractions, until your cervix starts to efface (to grow flatter and wider), you're not ready to give birth. But once that starts to happen, you'll know the moment is at hand. Your doctor will also take note of the placement of the baby. Up until the end, the baby is up high, around your abdomen. But near the time when you're going to give birth, the baby "drops," that is, the bump will get lower on your abdomen, which is another sign that you're almost due.

Another sign that you're close to giving birth is when your water breaks. When this happens, the sac that contains the fluid that your baby floats in ruptures, and it all comes pouring out of your vagina. If this happens at a time when you're not yet in labor and not feeling strong contractions, don't let that stop you from rushing to the hospital. Your baby needs that fluid, and even if you're not ready to deliver, your doctor will do whatever is necessary to bring your baby into the world.

Labor

Labor is a very appropriate name for this stage of your pregnancy, because it won't happen without a lot of effort on your part. Babies have been descending through the vaginal canal since time immemorial, so you have to accept that you can push a baby's head through your vagina. Just don't let anyone talk you into believing that it's going to be easy, because it's not.

Now, in general, women who've delivered a baby before have faster labors, and women who have their first baby have slower labors. Some women take twenty-four hours, and others take less than an hour, and there's no way to tell ahead of time what your labor will be like. From a psychological point of view, it's better not to think about it ahead of time and just accept whatever happens. There are couples who try to plan out everything, down to what music will be playing, but once you're in labor, you won't care about anything but pushing that baby out.

Cesarean Section

Not every woman can give birth vaginally. As I mentioned earlier, many women used to die in childbirth because of long labor or hemorrhaging, but today, if this happens, the situation is far from grave. Your doctor can make an incision in your abdomen and remove the baby safely. The main difference between giving birth this way and vaginally is that you'll have a scar in your uterus and on your skin and it will take longer to heal, although your vagina won't undergo any stretching and will not need any healing time at all. In addition, any future pregnancies will be different because of your cesarean section. Your baby may also look better, because a long labor, especially if forceps are required to help the baby through the vaginal canal, can make the heads of some newborns misshapen and bruised. Yet all of that doesn't matter because in a few weeks' time, you'll never know the difference.

There can be several reasons that your doctor will decide during labor that this delivery needs to be made via C-section; these include

- Something about your baby, such as the heart rate, indicates that the baby can't wait to be delivered vaginally.
- Your cervix stops dilating, making it impossible for the baby to come out vaginally.
- You have pushed for some time, and the baby did not move deeply enough through the birth canal.
- Your doctor detects that you have a herpes outbreak, which would pass to the baby during a vaginal delivery.

Some women and their doctors decide ahead of time that their babies are going to be delivered by a C-section.

The Top Ten Reasons for Having a C-Section

1. You've had a C-section or another uterine surgery before and are not a candidate for vaginal birth.
2. Your labor is too slow or it stops.
3. The baby shows signs of compromise that necessitate an expeditious delivery.
4. Your baby is in the wrong position, such as the breech position, that is, feet first, rather than head first, or transverse lie. Although a vaginal breech birth is possible, many doctors feel that it's safer to deliver such babies via C-section.
5. The baby is very large, making a vaginal birth risky or even impossible.
6. You develop placenta previa, which means that your placenta is covering the cervix, so that the baby can't go through it to enter the vaginal canal.
7. You're carrying more than one baby, and multiple births are considered too risky for vaginal delivery.

8. It's discovered that you or your baby has some medical condition that would make vaginal delivery too risky.

9. You have an outbreak of herpes.

10. Another reason is "cesarean delivery on maternal request," which means the mother requests a cesarean, but there are no specific medical or other indications.

Because of these possibilities, more than 30 percent of all deliveries in the United States are done via C-section these days, up from only 6 percent in 1970. Have matters changed medically to such a degree that so many more C-sections are being done? Probably. Here are some possible reasons for this rise in C-sections:

- Routine electronic fetal monitoring may increase the chances of having a cesarean.
- The number of epidurals being performed is higher, which may increase your chance of having a cesarean, although that's not completely clear.
- A prior cesarean section definitely increases the likelihood of your having a cesarean the next time.
- The higher IVF rate increases the number of cesarean sections performed because of the greater incidence of twins.
- Older mothers have a higher chance of having a cesarean section.
- Obese mothers have more cesarean sections.
- In some cases, doctors may be afraid that if something goes wrong during a vaginal birth they'll get sued, so they prefer to perform a C-section.

One factor that has changed is that doctors can now perform a C-section using a horizontal skin incision (the "bikini cut" or "Pfannenstiel incision") so that the resulting scar is much smaller and can be placed below the bikini line. In addition, anesthesia and surgical care have become better, and these advances mean that more women are open to having Cesarean sections, which allow them both to avoid the hard work of labor and to plan the exact date that they will give birth. These days, when mothers who work outside the home remain at the office until the last possible moment, such timing may be considered important.

Your partner will probably be allowed to stay in the operating room during a cesarean section, unless it is an emergency C-section, and there isn't enough time to have him get completely gowned. Also, if he reacts poorly in the operating room, he may be asked to stay outside.

Pregnancy Complications

Although it is common for a pregnant woman to experience some bleeding during her first trimester, this is not true for the second and third trimesters. If you experience any bleeding, report it to your doctor. It's important to judge how much you are bleeding, so try to keep track. Wear a pad that will help you do this. Do not insert anything in your vagina while you are bleeding, so don't use a tampon and don't have intercourse.

Sometimes intercourse can cause a woman to bleed. Because the cervix of a pregnant woman has bigger and more plentiful blood vessels, if the penis comes into contact with one, a little bleeding may occur. You might be tempted not to mention anything to your doctor if this happens, especially because pregnant couples are already a little afraid to have sex. If they feel that they might have endangered the pregnancy in any way because they've had sex, they'll feel especially guilty and are more likely to give up on having sex than talk to their doctor about the bleeding that occurred. The fact is that you are very unlikely to harm your baby by having sex, and this type of bleeding is not dangerous. But your doctor still needs to know about it, in case the timing of the bleeding during intercourse was only coincidental, and the true cause is something more serious.

It's amazing how much privacy you lose in the process of having a baby, so that you even have to share your sex life, but in the end, that can be a good thing. Too much inhibition isn't good for a couple's sex life, so if you lose some of those inhibitions during pregnancy, you may be able to put your newfound freedom from prudishness to good use later on.

Postpregnancy Care

It takes longer for you to heal from a C-section, because it's a relatively major surgical procedure. Yet no matter how you give birth, your body will soon recover. When it does, it's important to work on regaining your previous physical conditioning, the muscle tone and stamina you had before your pregnancy. If you've put on a lot of weight and are breast-feeding, some of it will come off naturally but not all of it. Although having a new baby is tiring and will seem like a lot of exercise, you'll need to begin working out again so that you stay healthy.

Breast-feeding is encouraged because it's healthier for both babies and mothers. If you have problems with breast-feeding, by all means let your doctor know about it, and consider talking to a lactation consultant.

You also need to make sure that you are psychologically healthy. Some new mothers get the blues, while others become severely depressed. The blues can be normal, but depression is not. Even though being a new mother is supposed to be one of the happiest times in a woman's life, anywhere from 10 to 20 percent of women will experience some symptoms of postpartum depression. A shocking fact is that 50 percent of women who have depression symptoms will experience major depression. Depression is hard to handle at any point during life, but the hormonal changes of being pregnant, combined with the duties of new motherhood, make depression even harder to bear. The following information will help you determine the difference between a simple pregnancy-induced hormonal imbalance and a more serious depression issue so that you will know what you are up against.

What Is Pregnancy Depression?

Pregnancy depression is the same as any other depression, in terms of being a mood disorder and a chemical imbalance. The only difference is that this depression occurs during or after pregnancy or is brought on by the hormones of the pregnancy itself.

If you are experiencing any of the following symptoms for two weeks or longer, you may have pregnancy depression and should talk with your doctor.

Signs of Pregnancy Depression

- Persistent sadness
- Difficulty sleeping, sleeping too much, or not sleeping enough
- Recurring thoughts of death or suicide
- Changes in eating habits
- Thoughts of hopelessness
- Loss of interest in activities you used to enjoy

Following is a list of things that could possibly cause the onset of a depression during pregnancy.

- Relationship issues
- Financial issues
- Pregnancy complications
- Previous pregnancy losses
- Fertility treatments
- Family history of depression

Treatment of Pregnancy Depression

Depending on the severity of the depression, your doctor has to decide whether it can be treated without medication or whether you do need medication. For mild forms of depression, here are several options that you and your doctor can use to help you.

- Support groups
- Private psychotherapy
- Light therapy

Many forms of depression will respond only to medication. Your doctor will choose a medication that's safe for both you and your baby. Not taking medication to treat the depression may be counterproductive because women who are depressed are less able to take good care of themselves and their babies.

Keep in mind that feeling sad from time to time or worrying about the baby is normal, and it will usually pass. You are not depressed if you have these feelings occasionally, due to either circumstance or hormones, and you should not worry excessively about being depressed. The depression becomes an issue only when these feelings do not go away, and you start to suffer because of them. If you think any of the symptoms in this section describe how you feel, you should definitely speak to your doctor right away.

If you become depressed, it's important to recognize it and combat it. If you wallow in sadness, it won't be good for your health, your baby's well-being, or your relationship with your partner. When you feel a flood of sadness coming on, do something to change your thoughts. Put on some lively music. Call your best friend who makes you laugh. Watch a sitcom. Strap your baby into a carrier and go for a fast walk. (Exercise causes your body to release endorphins that make you feel better.) Although I know that your new baby will occupy your mind most of the time, don't forget about your partner. Keep in mind that your relationship should last forever, long after your children will have gone off on their own, so while your partner can take care of himself physically, your mutual relationship needs tending, and that includes your sex life. You do have to wait for your doctor to give you the go-ahead for intercourse, but once that happens, no matter how tired you are and no matter how low your feelings of sexual arousal, make the effort to jump-start your sex life. It may take a little concentration on your part, but once you get it going again, it should do quite well on its own momentum. Yet getting that engine going can be difficult at first, so be prepared to put a little extra energy into that part of your life, and you'll ensure that your relationship will be there for you well into the future.

9

Perimenopause and Menopause

As I said earlier, at some point your ovaries will run out of follicles to turn into eggs to be released. When that happens, your monthly cycles will cease, which is called menopause. The cessation of your monthly cycle will bring some changes, which I'll get to in a bit. But before you reach menopause, your body will undergo other changes, and this period of your life is called perimenopause. The changes at the perimenopause state have less to do with the release of eggs, but rather with a decrease in the amount of hormones that your ovaries produce, specifically, estrogen, progesterone, and androgens. On average, this decrease in hormone production will start about four years before you reach menopause, but some women begin to sense these changes much earlier, in their late thirties, whereas other women don't become aware of any changes until a few months before they actually reach menopause. By the way, you are said to have reached menopause twelve months after your last period, so the entire year after your periods have ceased is part of perimenopause.

Why does it take so long for a woman to undergo this process? The answer might be found in looking at women who undergo instant menopause. If a woman has medical problems that require a complete hysterectomy, and her ovaries are removed, too, then she will undergo what is called surgical menopause. Instead of there being a gradual decrease in hormones, she'll go from having a full complement of hormones before surgery to almost none after surgery. It seems that these women suffer from all of the various symptoms of perimenopause (see the following section) but to a greater degree. So, the gradual hormonal decrease that takes place in perimenopause helps you adapt to the coming changes in your body and may also protect you from having worse symptoms.

Although symptoms such as hot flashes are generally considered to be a part of menopause, in actuality they begin during peri-menopause, and for many women, many of these symptoms will actually end when they are fully menopausal (although that's not true for all women). Once you start to detect some or all of these symptoms, you will know that you are in the perimenopausal state of your life.

The Top Ten Symptoms of Perimenopause

You should report any changes to your doctor because although you may assume that what's happening to you is simply routine, it might not be. In addition, your doctor may be able to provide you with relief from some of these symptoms. Because the symptoms can begin years before you reach menopause and can continue afterward, it's certainly a good idea to check with your doctor to see whether you can do anything to minimize or even eliminate any negative effects.

1. **Irregular bleeding** is the one symptom, out of all of them, that you should most definitely report to your doctor. Irregular bleeding can include many different variations, such as irregular periods, an increased or decreased flow during your period, and spotting at other times. All of these could be a result of your changing hormones, but they could also signify something else. Only your doctor will be able to tell, and that's why you must report these symptoms to make sure that they are part of the normal changes that occur during this time and are not being caused by anything else. Just because you're in perimenopause doesn't mean that you can't develop a uterine fibroid, for example, so don't make the mistake of assuming that any changes in your menstrual habits are simply due to the aging process.

2. **Hot flashes** are the symptom that everybody connects to menopause. For some women, they can be very annoying, but for most women, hot flashes aren't that bad. Some women never get them at all, while other women experience them for only a brief time. Getting rid of hot flashes used to be the main reason that women took hormone replacement therapy (HRT). But because of the risks, the routine use of HRT has stopped. Instead, doctors prescribe HRT only when women have severe symptoms and its benefits outweigh the risks (more on HRT in a bit).

3. **Breast tenderness** may be something that you remember from when you were first pregnant, and here you are, so many years later, and you find yourself facing the same issue. All of these conditions have to do with changes in your hormone levels. If you're in perimenopause, you shouldn't be surprised to find your body undergoing a change of some sort.

Breast tenderness during perimenopause and menopause is not one of the symptoms that gets very much attention, but one possible consequence is that this tenderness means your breasts are suddenly off limits to your sex partner. This can be very frustrating to the man, for whom touching his partner's breasts was an important part of becoming aroused, especially if this restriction comes at a time when he himself is already having some difficulties in that department. There are also women who require breast stimulation to become aroused themselves. For them, the issue of breast tenderness can be very problematic. If both partners end up getting mad at each other for this change in their sexual habits, which is beyond their control, that could be the biggest problem of all.

Increased communication with your partner is the key to preventing any harm to your sex life caused by the issue of breast tenderness and most problems in the sexual arena. Talk about what these changes to your breasts are doing to your sex life. Make sure that your partner knows this isn't something you thought up as an excuse not to have sex but is actually a common symptom of entering menopause. Just don't have such a conversation in the bedroom, especially if you're trying to have sex. In coming to a solution, ideally you might find other parts of your bodies that will have a similar erotic effect (and simply looking for them will perk up your sex life in the short run). If you can share in this experience and use it to bring yourselves closer, rather than let it become a wedge that drives you apart, you can definitely mitigate the effects these changes have on your sex life. Even if you don't find the perfect solution, hopefully you will end up with a relationship that remains sexually fulfilling nevertheless.

4. **Premenstrual syndrome** (PMS) is a condition that affects some women more than others. Many women never experience any changes prior to the start of their menses, while others have symptoms that can be truly debilitating. The range of symptoms goes from the physical (such as backache, headache, and cramping) to the psychological (forgetfulness, irritability, and fatigue).

If you suspect that you have PMS, write down your symptoms as they occur. Keep a log for a period of several months so that you can describe to your doctor exactly what's been happening to you. The more information your doctor has, the more likely he or she will be able to help you. This is also true if your symptoms suddenly worsen as you enter perimenopause.

5. The cause of increased **fatigue** can be physical or mental. If you're feeling depressed, that will tend to drain you of much-needed energy. Believe it or not, one of the best things you can do to reduce these feelings is to exercise (assuming there is no underlying physical ailment that is making you feel tired). Exercise causes your body to release endorphins, which will elevate your mood and thus reduce fatigue. Several medications can also help with your PMS symptoms. Your doctor can help you find the best treatment for you.

6. **Vaginal dryness** can begin with a simple reduction of lubrication when you are sexually aroused and can progress to a point where your vagina becomes very dry and easily irritated, so that intercourse can go from being mildly uncomfortable to painful and can result in abrasion and bleeding. In addition to producing less lubrication after menopause, the tissues that make up your vagina get thinner and become less elastic (after all, your vagina no longer needs to stretch to allow a baby to get through). These changes can also make sex less comfortable and even painful.

Many young men complain that they ejaculate too quickly (what is called premature ejaculation). As a man ages, he's likely to lose this problem and may well end up with the reverse condition, so that it takes an extralong period of intercourse for him to have an orgasm. If this change occurs at the same time that his partner is suffering from vaginal dryness, the added time taken for intercourse can make her vagina feel even sorer after intercourse.

The cure for vaginal dryness is using an artificial lubricant, but don't assume that one application will do the trick. If you are very dry, and he is taking quite a long while, you'll probably have to apply the lubricant one or two more times. Because your partner may be afraid that removing his penis from your vagina will cause him to lose concentration and maybe even lose his erection, this can become a cause of conflict. If you're in that situation, don't fight with him, but instead make sure that the lubricant is within easy reach and simply put some on your hand and apply it to his penis as it is sliding in and out of you. Not only will this save you from needless discomfort, but he may even find that the process adds to his excitement and decreases the time he needs to have an orgasm.

Although routine hormone replacement (HRT) for all women in menopause is not recommended anymore because of the potential health risks, HRT in a localized version is available and can relieve severe menopausal symptoms such as vaginal dryness, using a much lower dose of estrogen.

One reason to consider this treatment is that vaginal lubrication, in addition to facilitating sex, is also a sign of sexual arousal. Some women who stop lubricating become unsure of whether they are aroused, and the dryness also makes it more difficult for their partners to tell. If a dose of hormones applied to the vagina can solve this problem, you and your doctor might decide that it's the right treatment for you.

7. **Sleeping difficulties** can sometimes stem from hot flashes that wake you up in the middle of the night and then don't allow you to fall back to sleep, or else they can come from your having to get up several times to go to the toilet. Or maybe they simply cause havoc in your life with no rhyme or reason. It's better to try nonmedical remedies first, such as exercise, staying away from caffeine, and not going to bed until you are just about ready to fall asleep, but if nothing works for you, ask your doctor to see what else might be available.

Whether you're having problems sleeping because of menopause or because your partner is snoring away half of the night, if you have a spare bedroom (and many older couples whose children have left home do have an extra bedroom or two), use it. First, it will help you avoid unnecessary conflicts, because interfering with your partner's sleep time when you could avoid doing so will not make you very popular. If you're up because you can't sleep but are just lying there in bed in order not to disturb your partner, that will make it even more difficult for you to go back to sleep. Maybe you need to turn on the light and read for twenty minutes or so or change the room temperature in some way. Whatever it is, if you have the luxury of added privacy in a separate room, staying up will be a little less stressful if you can do it on your own.

8. **Frequent urination** is another symptom caused by a diminishing of your hormones. One of estrogen's many duties is to maintain your bladder and urethra in a healthy condition. When your levels of estrogen begin to drop in perimenopause and menopause, one result is a weakening in these parts of the body. As a result, you may find that you have to go to the toilet more often or that you leak urine at certain times, such as when you cough or sneeze.

The main thing that you can do for yourself is practice Kegel exercises. To perform these, you tighten and loosen your puboccygeus muscles. You say you don't know which muscles those are? Of course, you do, you probably have just never heard the name. They're the muscles you use when you stop your flow of urine. Once you've identified them, you'll see that it's easy to tighten them at other times. You can start these exercises by doing a few sets of three repetitions and build up to a point when you can do three sets of ten or more. As these muscles tighten, you'll gain more control over your need to urinate.

By practicing Kegel exercises, you'll also be able to tighten your vagina around your partner's penis, which may cause sensations that he will enjoy. You can do Kegels everywhere, because no one can see what you're doing. I sometimes suggest to women that they do them while they're driving and have stopped at a red light.

9. **Mood swings** can also occur in this time of life. They might arise as a result of other symptoms; for example, if you're extra tired because you're not sleeping well, that will make you grouchy. Or else the mood swings may be caused entirely by the changes in your

hormones. It's important to try to judge what exactly is happening to you. If you feel sad because of an actual symptom, it may be easier to overcome that on your own than it is if you feel depressed because of a drop in hormone levels, which you can't control.

10. **Changes in your sex drive** can also be a consequence of menopause. There are women who assume that when they enter menopause, their sex lives are over, and with such thinking, you can almost guarantee that it will come true. On the other hand, some women discover that without the risk of pregnancy and with no interruptions because of "that time of the month," their sex lives blossom. It may also help if their children are gone, and the couple has added privacy.

There's that phrase, "Use it or lose it," and although it's not always true, what is true is if you stop having sex at this time of your life, your sex life will come to an end. But if you do whatever is necessary to keep your sex life in good health, then there's no reason for it to end. In other words, it's up to you.

In my opinion, many of the women who give up on sex when they hit menopause do so because they never got sexual satisfaction before this stage in their lives. If they weren't really enjoying good sex lives with their partners, then menopause became the excuse they were long hoping for. A woman who has had regular orgasms for her entire life, however, is not going to give up on sex without a fight. She'll find a way to compensate for any difficulties thrown her way by menopause, such as vaginal dryness, and will continue to have sex and have orgasms for decades to come.

Is Hormone Replacement Therapy for You?

Why can't the medical community decide whether hormone replacement therapy is good or bad? It's true that there was a revolution in thinking on HRT by the medical community,

From Dr. Amos's Office: Hormone Replacement Therapy

Hormone replacement therapy (HRT) consists of one or more of the following hormones: estrogens, progesterone, and sometimes testosterone. It can be given via tablets, patches, creams, vaginal rings, gels, or injection.

Today, HRT in menopausal women should mainly be given only for short-term relief (less than two years) from menopausal symptoms such as severe hot flashes or irregular bleeding. Patients need to make an informed choice and know about all of the benefits and the risks. Normal menopausal women with symptoms should take HRT treatment only at the lowest feasible therapeutic dose and for no longer than necessary. Other medications can be taken as an alternative to HRT; they include SSRIs (selective serotonin reuptake inhibitors) and neurontin.

Certain menopausal health problems, such as osteoporosis, can now be treated without HRT, and additional efforts may include exercise, diet improvements, and other lifestyle changes.

Younger women who have undergone surgical menopause or those with premature ovarian failure can safely use HRT for longer time periods.

Recent studies have shown that HRT taken soon after menopause may help protect against dementia, and HRT may actually prevent the development of heart disease and reduce the incidence of heart attacks in women between fifty and fifty-nine but not for older women. There is still an increased risk of breast cancer, although one recent study showed that the increased breast cancer risk applies only to women who take certain progesterone preparations but not to those taking progesterone itself.

Women who have taken HRT and then stopped want to know whether they've increased their risks forever or only for a short time. Regarding the increased risk of breast cancer, it seems that there is a two-year window after a woman stops taking HRT when an elevated risk remains, but then it disappears. For cardiovascular issues, as soon as a woman stops taking HRT, the risk fades away.

but it didn't arise out of bad faith. Patients were coming to their doctors with the list of complaints I've described previously, and doctors wanted to help alleviate these symptoms. HRT seemed to be able to do that, while at the same time diminishing the risks of developing breast cancer and heart disease. Or, at least, that's the way it seemed, according to the studies available at the time. Yet then some long-term studies showed that HRT actually increased the risk of breast cancer and cardiovascular problems, so the medical community put the brakes on.

Aging Gracefully

In the early 1960s, hormone replacement therapy was touted as being a fountain of youth for menopausal women. Doctors prescribed it almost indiscriminately, and the high doses of estrogen did create an illusion of youth in older women. Their skin became moister, firmer, and plumper and problems with vaginal dryness lessened. Yet this came with a price, as was revealed by long-term medical studies that began to warn of the risks of HRT. Nowadays, even though modern women still have the normal amount of female vanity, most of them don't want to take a chance on using HRT simply to look younger.

In any discussion of why a woman's sex drive might diminish as she hits menopause, let's not forget an important component: body image. We are all bombarded with images of young women on TV, in movies, and in magazines, and rarely do we see older women. For the most part, if you do see an older woman in the media, any signs of aging are airbrushed away. The truth, of course, is that as both men and women age, their bodies change. And when you're ready for sex, that is, when you're naked, those changes stand out even more.

The mistake that many women make is to go into hiding. Where they once proudly showed off their bodies to their partners, suddenly they're always under some sort of wrap. The problem is that when a woman reaches an age where she doesn't find her body as appealing when she looks in the mirror, her male partner is also changing. He now needs more stimulation to become aroused, rather than less, and remember, visual stimulation is very important to a man.

While there may be no ideal solution, the best is a compromise. If you feel that you want to cover up your body, and he prefers that you do not, make a point of covering up with something sexy, rather than with an old flannel nightgown. If there are parts of your body that you still like, show them off. And the parts you want to cover will look better under see-through lace than if you wear a ratty old T-shirt.

Why is it that so many older men run off with younger women? While this book is supposed to cover the knowledge base of a gynecologist, here I have to diverge a bit and go into the male realm, although I promise that this also has to do with you. A woman's hot flashes are visible, so they're a common-enough subject, but the early changes that a man goes through, before he may have any actual erectile difficulties, are invisible. Young men have what are called psychogenic erections, which means if they see or think about something that they feel is sexy, their penises will become erect. At a certain age—which, depending on the man, could begin in his forties, fifties, or sixties—a man loses the ability to have psychogenic erections. Instead, he requires physical stimulation to become erect. But if he doesn't know this, and neither does his female partner, that can cause problems. As I've just discussed regarding body image, a woman who was used to seeing her husband's penis pop up when she walked around naked will feel badly about herself when this stops happening. She'll either blame herself or maybe jump to the conclusion that he's having an affair, and as a consequence, she'll withdraw from him sexually. He may also believe that because his wife doesn't look the way she did when she was twenty, his penis no longer gets hard when he sees her naked. So, what's his solution? To find a younger woman.

Once you know the cause of this, you can predict what will happen. True, if he's in a new relationship with a younger woman, his penis will probably react in a positive manner. He will most likely find himself having those psychogenic erections once again. The question is, for how long? The underlying physical changes won't have diminished, so there will soon come a day when this new love of his life will no longer be able to produce the same psychogenic erections that she once could. And he may well have thrown out a very good marriage, damaged his relationship with his children, and saddled himself with paying divorce lawyers and settlements, all in a cause that was ultimately hopeless. So, the more that older couples understand about what is happening to them, the better choices they will make.

Osteoporosis and How to Prevent It

Osteoporosis is a condition in which a person's bones thin out and become less dense. Although it can and does happen to both sexes, women usually suffer from it earlier than men, and it is often triggered by menopause, so it is a disease that is more commonly associated with women. In fact, one out of five women older than age fifty has osteoporosis, which means at some point in their lives 50 percent of them will suffer from a bone fracture.

Your skeleton is obviously key to your well-being. A woman who has osteoporosis will experience added pain, most often lower back pain, due to spinal discs that break or fracture and lead to eventual deformities, such as curvature of the spine, which could be moderate to quite severe. Osteoporosis also increases the risk of having other bones break, such as the hip bone, either as a result of a fall or simply on their own. If a woman with osteoporosis does fall, she is much more likely to break a bone. Osteoporosis is one of the leading causes of people being admitted to nursing homes.

Your bones are made from calcium and phosphate, and if you haven't been getting enough of these essential building ingredients, then over time your bones will suffer. That is why it is so important that younger women make sure they get enough calcium in their diets. The recommended amount of calcium is 1,200 milligrams a day and another 800 to 1,000 international units of vitamin D3. You can get this dosage from eating the right foods, which includes drinking low-fat milk and eating other dairy products, such as cheese and yogurt; eating green leafy vegetables, such as spinach and kale; and eating fish, such as salmon and sardines (with the bones).

Most women who are diagnosed with osteoporosis don't know it until they end up breaking a bone. It is therefore vital that you see your doctor so that you can be tested for osteoporosis before you suffer any damage. A bone-density test is an important tool in diagnosing osteoporosis and protecting women from its effects.

If you already have osteoporosis, you must take extra precautions against sustaining a fall. Make sure that the place where you live isn't cluttered with objects that you could trip over. Remember that bathrooms can be dangerous, so have safety bars installed in your tub or shower. Don't be too proud to use a cane when walking outside on streets that could have a lot of cracks. Always wear comfortable shoes that promote good balance, as opposed to high heels. And if the weather conditions are such that the risks of falling are high, either stay indoors or if you must go out, do so only when accompanied by someone else.

One of the reasons given for taking HRT was as a supposed protection against osteoporosis. Yet it seems that this protection lasted for only about six or seven years. On the other hand, many women who took HRT for hot flashes and other symptoms found that once they stopped taking HRT, those symptoms didn't return (although they might have disappeared in any case). Today, possible HRT risks outweigh the potential osteoporosis risk, and HRT should not be given to prevent osteoporosis.

Whether the risks posed by HRT outweigh the benefits is something that you will have to discuss with your doctor.

The question of HRT is a very complicated one, and many factors must be considered. For women with a family history of

From Dr. Amos's Office: Osteoporosis

You've undoubtedly seen the many commercials for various drugs to combat osteoporosis. Although these drugs offer some protection, the FDA has told drug manufacturers that they are exaggerating the benefits of their products. That's not to say that you shouldn't take any of these drugs, but because there are also possible side effects, you should first discuss this with your doctor.

On the other hand, certain forms of exercise, such as weight lifting, stair climbing, and running, do work, and they have only positive side effects. These activities are proven bone builders, plus they protect you against other diseases. They also make you feel better about yourself, because they improve your appearance and help you maintain your weight. By the way, for women younger than seventy-five, osteoporosis is a bigger problem than for men, but by age seventy-five it becomes equally problematic for both sexes, so you should encourage any older men you know who are leading sedentary lifestyles to join you in your exercise program.

osteoporosis, the risks posed by HRT must be weighed seriously against the protection that it offers.

One possible alternative to HRT is to take low-dosage birth control pills. They seem capable of alleviating some of the most uncomfortable symptoms, such as hot flashes, without posing the same risks as HRT, unless you are a smoker. Then there are the supposedly natural products made from soy or other ingredients that have been touted by an assortment of celebrities. The problem with these is that they really are untested. Because they're not drugs, the FDA doesn't get involved, so nobody really knows what the long-term side effects might be. Women have been going through menopause since time immemorial (at least, those who survived long enough to reach that stage of life), and they have done so without any drugs, so certainly one option is simply to try to cope the best you can so that you're not taking any unnecessary risks. Many women report that by increasing the amount of exercise they do and by losing weight, they've been able to reduce their menopausal symptoms. Whether or not this will help you in terms of alleviating your symptoms, it certainly is a positive life-style change worth trying.

If you're a twin, a study discovered that your odds of having a premature menopause, as early as forty years of age, are significantly greater. Oddly, only one of the two in a set of twins will experience premature menopause, while the other will have menopause at a more normal age. Scientists don't know for sure why this is, but perhaps as they work at discovering the cause, they'll also make a breakthrough in the treatment for menopause.

Are those of you who haven't gone through menopause still dreading it? I hope not, because as I've tried to show here, a lot of good comes with this new chapter in your life.

10

Enjoy Your Body
at Any Age

I am always deluged with questions, and in this chapter, I'll go over some of the topics I am frequently asked about, including loss of desire, how to integrate sex toys into your love life, and anal sex.

At the beginning of this book, I said that what made this book different from other books was its focus on sexuality. The reason this is necessary is that too many gynecologists and doctors of every sort don't have the training or the experience to help their patients function optimally when it comes to sex. I'm sure that so far, you've learned some important things about your sexuality.

The big difference between some of the problems that arise in a woman's sexual health and any other problems she might have is that sex is, for the most part, shared with another human being. Obviously, if you break a leg, it's going to have an impact on your partner, but you both share sex throughout your entire life together, which makes it very hard sometimes to separate sexual problems from relational ones. In fact, that's often the toughest part of my job—figuring out whether a specific problem being presented to me by a couple in my office exists because of an underlying relationship problem.

If a couple comes to my office, and they're fighting from the moment they walk through the door, then it's easy to predict that their sexual problems are based on their relationship issues. But if they say that they get along great, and from what I can see, they do, then I have to play detective to discover what the underlying issues may be.

If you are not seeing a professional counselor of any sort, try to play detective on your own. Maybe you won't be able to spot the source of any relationship troubles because you're too close to the situation, but then again, it may be obvious once you stop and examine your relationship. After you've identified what's wrong, you have the opportunity to make repairs. But if you remain ignorant, then the problem, whatever it is, will only grow worse.

In the chapter on STDs, I hope you noticed how many people have some type of an STD and don't know it because there are no outward signs. The very same thing can occur with sexual problems. The couple appear to be loving and have a great relationship, but when it comes to their sex lives, there is definitely a problem. She may claim to have low libido, and there are times when the cause is hormonal. There are other times when it's psychological. And, of course, occasionally it's a combination of both.

If you suddenly lost your appetite for food and were losing weight, you'd be concerned and would probably talk to your doctor about it. If you're like most of us, you'd start to worry that you had a serious illness, so you'd go to the doctor to have it checked out. Yet for many women, a loss of appetite for sex doesn't have the same priority. Sex is considered secondary, so the problem might be pushed under the rug.

As you can imagine, I strongly believe that's a big mistake. I've seen how unhappy a person with no sex life can be. It can wreck his or her relationships and lead to depression and all sorts of other issues. Although your physical wellness is obviously very important, so is your sexual wellness. It's important that you can count on your gynecologist to help you achieve the level of sexual health you deserve.

It's often difficult to get to the bottom of a problem on your own. Having the assistance of a sex therapist, a marital counselor, a social worker, or a religious leader can make a big difference. If you need a reference, don't hesitate to ask your gynecologist.

There is no doubt that your hormones play an important role in your sex life. Some women have serious problems with their hormones that wreak havoc with their sex lives. Yet for every one of those, there are ten others who blame their hormones for ruining their sex lives when in fact that's not the case at all.

By the way, I'm not talking only about menopausal women. Some young women also undergo significant changes in their hormones every month. Being pregnant also affects your hormone levels, as does stress, which is all around us in both psychological and physical forms. Yet you need to keep in mind that although your hormones are important in generating arousal, they are not required for you to actually become aroused. You can become aroused despite any changes in your hormones, but that will

---

From Dr. Amos's Office: Enjoying Your Sex Life

I have had women come to me with a variety of complaints, mostly minor, and it's obvious that their overall level of satisfaction with life is low. With some of these women, I discover that underlying everything is a problem with their sex lives. If I can help them overcome that (and because I'm willing to probe, I usually can), the change in their overall outlook can be dramatic.

occur only if you believe it will and then set out to make it happen.

Let me be as clear as I can about this. At the beginning of your relationship with your partner, you probably started to get feelings of sexual arousal, you either initiated sexual contact or agreed to a sexual episode initiated by your partner, and you had a great time making love to each other. Then, for some reason, those feelings of arousal suddenly disappeared, and because you'd never had sex without that signal of arousal, you adopted the attitude that you *shouldn't* have sex without that signal. If your partner indicated that he wants sex, you turned him down. Or else you agreed to have sex just to please him, but your attitude was very negative, and you ended up getting little or no enjoyment from it. What I'm saying is, if there are no good reasons within the relationship for this lack of arousal, and your relationship is apparently fine, the cause may be changes in your hormones. In such a case, you should push any negative thoughts aside and have sex despite the lack of sexual arousal. I'm predicting that most of the time, once you begin, your level of arousal will grow, and you'll end up enjoying yourself.

I'm not saying you need to do this if your level of arousal fails you from time to time. But when months go by, and you don't get that signal, and you're not having sex, that can have an effect on your overall relationship, especially if your partner still wants sex as much as ever.

Your attitude is the key for this to be successful. If you resent your partner for wanting to initiate sex, even if you actually go along, then the likelihood of your becoming aroused diminishes greatly. But if you agree to have sex with a positive attitude, then the likelihood of your level of sexual arousal climbing while you're cuddling and caressing each other increases dramatically, and the odds are that when all is said and done, you'll be quite glad that you went ahead and made love.

What you must do for this to be successful is tuck the following little piece of information into your brain and remember it from time to time: the fact that having sex without first being aroused can be wonderful. Let me explain why. Women take longer to become aroused than men. I tell men not to bring flowers with them but to send the flowers ahead of time. Those flowers will act as a catalyst, awakening the woman's sexual arousal a little more each time she steals a glance at them. By the time she sees the man later on, those flowers should have made her feel sexually aroused, at least to a certain degree. If, for some reason, things that once triggered sexual arousal in you—flowers, watching him shave in the morning, or seeing him change the baby's diaper—no longer have that effect, you can't let this have a negative impact on your sex life or your relationship. If you allow yourself to get sad or angry or frustrated, that will make it all the much harder to become sexually aroused during sex. So when you start to get such feelings, I want you to reach back and pull out the memories of some wonderful sexual episodes that took place despite your initial lack of desire. Use them to turn aside any negative feelings.

There are several aspects to all of this. Obviously, having orgasms prevents you from feeling sexually frustrated. And even though you don't seem to have those old feelings of arousal that were once so common, that doesn't mean you can't still be sexually frustrated. Yet in addition to orgasms, you get many other pleasures from having sex: the feelings of closeness that develop between you and your partner; the sensuous feelings of touching each other and intertwining your naked bodies; the wonderful memories that sex evokes and the intimacy it creates. By giving up on having sex because you don't feel aroused, you're giving up not only on orgasms but also on all of those other aspects of a sexual relationship. The price you pay for avoiding sex because you don't become aroused is truly a very high one.

I understand that if you've normally engaged in sex only when you became aroused, it can be confusing to suddenly agree to have sex when you're not aroused. Without that early warning signal, there will probably be times when you have sex and never become aroused. Maybe you didn't have a terrible day at the office, but a few little workday incidents remain sufficiently annoying to keep you from becoming aroused. If that happens, I would tell you to satisfy your partner, enjoy the cuddling and touching, and not worry about the fact that you don't have an orgasm. As long as you do become aroused from initiating sex from time to time, that's all that matters. Your sex life will not evaporate entirely just because this one aspect of it, arousal leading to sex, is no longer completely operative.

Of course, having a positive outlook about your sex life is important, whether or not your hormones may be affecting it, but that positive outlook may not come naturally. You might have to give it a boost from time to time.

If sex is natural, why would you need to try to artificially enhance your attitude? On one hand, women have made great strides in the last fifty years. The birth control pill has freed them from the worry of unintended pregnancy. Information about how to have orgasms is readily available. And many men have received the message that it is important for them to consider their partners' sexual satisfaction. Yet with so many women now in the workforce, the level of stress that many of them are under has grown considerably. Time to think about sex and romance during the day has, in the meantime, shrunk dramatically. And the distractions—TV, computers, iPods, and so on—have also taken away from everyone's time to simply daydream. Yet daydreaming about sex is fundamental to a woman's sexual arousal.

Sex Toys

The term *sex toy* is not one I prefer to use, but because it is so commonly applied to these items, there's no point in fighting it. When it is an item that merely gives pleasure to the couple, such as body paints, the term could be appropriate, but with some of these items, such as a vibrator, which may be a woman's only means of achieving sexual satisfaction, then it is certainly not a toy but an important tool. So, in this section, we'll look at what are called sex toys and go over some of the pertinent facts as they might apply to a gynecologist.

I'll begin with the most common, which is the vibrator. As I've said before, there are women who cannot have an orgasm without the very strong sensations created by a vibrator. For some women, a battery-operated vibrator can produce sufficiently intense sensations, whereas others require the more powerful motor of a machine that plugs into the wall. The problem with vibrators is that women can become hooked on them because no man can even come close to being able to duplicate the sensations provided by a vibrator. If a woman is having problems reaching orgasms by other means, then it is definitely appropriate to use a vibrator. If she doesn't have such problems but is without a partner and from time to time would like to employ a vibrator, that's fine, too. But if she begins to use a vibrator every time she masturbates while single, she may discover that she then cannot have orgasms with a partner, and that could present a host of problems.

Some women react negatively to the very idea of masturbation for a variety of different reasons, many of which have to do with their upbringing. Most young children will touch their genitals because, quite simply, it's pleasurable. The touching of one's genitals is not something that we do publicly, and parents are right to pass on to children the message that it's only to be done in private. Yet many parents instead give the message that it's wrong altogether, and they are quite emphatic about it, so much so that when the child grows up into an adult, the taboo against masturbation remains strong. For a woman who finds a partner who gives her sexual satisfaction, this is not a problem. There's no law that says anyone has to masturbate. Men tend to masturbate more than women do, and in part that's due to the fact that they handle their genitals more. But if a woman cannot have orgasms with a partner, then learning how to masturbate could be the only way that she can develop the ability to have orgasms and then, hopefully, pass that knowledge on to a partner.

This is where a doctor—in particular, a gynecologist—comes in. If a woman who has never masturbated is told by her doctor that she should try to masturbate in order to learn how to have orgasms, then she is much more likely to do so than she would on her own. But, of course, first she has to tell her doctor about this problem. In many cases, the type of woman who refrains from masturbation is also the type of woman who is least likely to talk about her sex life with her gynecologist, and sensing that reticence, most gynecologists won't press these women for information.

Obviously, this is a mistake on the part of both the patient and the doctor. Whether any of you readers who are in that predicament will change this situation as a result of reading this book, I don't know. Yet there is another solution, which is to make an appointment with a sex therapist. A sex therapist is used to talking about sex, and a sex therapist can also make the connection with your gynecologist, reporting on what your condition is (only if you allow this, of course), thus opening up future dialogues between you and your gynecologist.

I often quote the mythical Victorian mother who, when discussing the issue of sex with her daughter on the night before her wedding, is purported to have told her, "Just lie back and think of England." Even today, it's absolutely true that for hundreds of millions of women around the world, sex is only for the man's enjoyment. (There are reportedly 130 million women in Africa alone who have undergone female genital cutting or female genital mutilation that makes it very difficult or impossible for them to have orgasms.) Why is it so important that a woman have orgasms? For centuries, a large percentage of Chinese women had their feet bound when they were children, and they were never able to walk normally again. That people, both men and women, have needlessly subjugated themselves to pain and suffering in so many different ways because of social pressures doesn't make any of this right. A woman is born with a clitoris, she is capable of having orgasms, orgasms bring sexual release and pleasure, and there's not one good reason that women shouldn't have orgasms, any more than they shouldn't be able to see, smell, and taste. If you get pleasure from eating a well-prepared meal or seeing a beautiful sunset or smelling a flower, why shouldn't you also get pleasure from having sex with your partner? The attitude that women don't need to have orgasms should be put to rest, alongside the ideas that women shouldn't have the right to vote or aren't entitled to equal pay.

Basically, I am saying that the inability to have an orgasm is a medical issue (whether it is physical or psychological) and that you should have the courage to talk to your gynecologist about this. If the two of you agree, you should purchase a vibrator in order to learn how to become orgasmic. If you want to know more about this whole subject in detail, I suggest that you buy my book *Sex for Dummies*.

As for other sex toys, if you have a question about any that you want to use or that your partner is suggesting that you incorporate into your sex life, ask your doctor. One reason for doing this could be that if your partner is suggesting the use of some toy or position that you instinctively find not to your liking but are unsure of how to turn this request down, your doctor may provide you with the perfect excuse, which is that it's not safe. You don't need a prescription from your doctor to say no to any sex act that you don't want to do, but if you have a partner who is very persistent, then having your gynecologist as an ally could be very useful.

Anal Sex

More and more people are engaging in anal sex and anal play these days. Anal sex usually involves putting a penis into the anus, but it can also involve other sexual acts, such as placing one or more fingers, the tongue, or some sort of sex toy into the anus. Anal sex is sometimes performed because of the low risk of unwanted pregnancy, and sometimes it's done because, technically, the woman thinks she is still a virgin when the vagina is not penetrated.

Anal sex can be pleasurable for both men and women, but it is also associated with a manifold increase of health risks. The two major risks associated with anal sex are physical injury and infections.

Although the vagina was designed to receive a penis, the anus wasn't. The anus is usually tighter than the vagina, so there is an increased risk of tearing. This tearing can lead to bleeding, infection, pain, and permanent damage of the rectal tissue. Good lubrication during anal intercourse could decrease the risk of these injuries. On the other hand, recent studies have shown that lubricants can affect the ability of the lining of the anus to fight infection, so now there are new risks.

There is also an increased risk of infections because the anus is host to a significant amount of potentially harmful microbes, thus making the transmission of disease much easier. Some of the organisms that cause these increased risks are HIV, herpes, human papilloma virus (HPV), gonorrhea, chlamydia, and hepatitis A and B. In addition, anal sex is associated with an increased risk of anal cancer, most likely because of transmission of the HPV virus.

Using condoms during anal sex can significantly decrease the risk of infection transmission, although you have to bear in mind that condoms can break or fall off. Another potential danger is the risk that germs from your intestines will be carried into your vagina if you first insert the penis into the rectum and then into the vagina. Couples practicing anal sex have to be very careful to avoid any such contamination. If you want to have vaginal penetration right after anal sex, it's best to use different condoms and also cleanse the penis prior to having vaginal sex.

Certainly, if you find that anal sex causes you any pain, you should not continue. Rather than be embarrassed to talk to your doctor about situations like this, you should instead use your doctor as an ally.

Vaginal Dryness

If your ability to become aroused decreases because of a change in your hormones brought on by perimenopause and menopause, there will be other accompanying symptoms, such as vaginal dryness. I wrote about this in chapter 9, and if for some reason you skipped that section, I recommend that you go back to it. Yet I also want to add something here about this important issue.

Vaginal dryness isn't something that sneaks up on you. Every woman knows that as she goes through menopause, she'll encounter issues with vaginal dryness, so it's a topic of conversation that you and your partner should discuss ahead of time. Similarly, you should talk about the consequences of aging on men with regard to sex: the changes in a man's ability to have an erection and a potential lessening of his desire because of a drop in the level of male sex hormones. Why should you discuss it ahead of time? Because these types of symptoms rarely occur overnight but build up gradually. Because these are signs of aging, rather than admit to them when they begin, many people give in to vanity and hide them. A woman suffering from a little vaginal dryness may accept the pain and might even fake orgasms. A man whose penis doesn't become erect on its own may, under the covers, give himself enough physical stimulation so that he becomes fully erect. If this pattern sets in, rather than learning how to adapt to these physical changes, a couple might suddenly find themselves having sex less often as both partners try to hide the fact from each other that they're growing older. This is foolish and avoidable.

If you talk about these issues ahead of time and maybe even decide how you're going to handle them, then when they begin to affect your sex life, you can admit to them readily and take the necessary actions. You won't need to hide these changes from each other because you'll have the confidence that comes from knowing that you already talked about them.

Maintaining a Healthy Sex Life

As I said a little earlier, a man should send flowers ahead of time so that they can work their magic over a longer time period. Yet women can help themselves greatly in the area of sexual arousal by stopping now and then to think romantic and sexy thoughts. If they can keep their level of arousal simmering, then when it comes time

---

From Dr. Amos's Office: Making Sex a Priority

I've mentioned how little time doctors have for their patients, but what is also true is how little time patients have for their doctors. If many doctors don't talk to their patients about sex, it's often because it is quite clear that a woman has shoehorned her visit between ten other items on her to-do list, and she is quite anxious to leave the doctor's office. Her mind is on the next five things she has to do, not on her sex life. Even if she wants to talk about it, she doesn't have time.

If you and your partner barely communicate until dinner time, and you get up at the crack of dawn, and your mind is focused on what that dawn is going to bring, then your sex life won't be simmering—it will be in a ziplock container at the back of the freezer. That is something you cannot allow. I want you to add an item to your to-do list: to remember that every now and then, during the day, you will think about sex. Just spend a minute or two recalling a past sexual episode and the feelings that it brought up. Raise the temperature of your libido by just a few degrees. I promise that these few minutes will pay strong dividends toward improving your sex life, which in turn will enhance your overall relationship.

to bring it to a boil, they'll find it a lot easier. But if they allow their sexual desire to get stone cold, then they'll need a lot more energy to get it going.

You also have to fit in some time to communicate with your partner. Just as you shouldn't allow the fires of your libido to die down entirely, you shouldn't let communications between you and your partner become too infrequent, either. I'm not saying that you need to hear from each other every hour, although these days, with e-mail and texting, it's possible to do just that with not much effort and without taking up much time. Yet it becomes a lot harder to reconnect physically if you and he barely communicate at other times.

This is similar to the advice I gave about considering your gynecologist your primary care physician. If you see your gynecologist with some frequency, undergoing the pelvic exam will be a lot easier than if you visit him or her only once a year. The more the lines of communication are open, the easier your interactions will be.

Your Right to Good Sex

Finally, never forget that you have every right to have a satisfying sex life. Because of the remnants of the Puritan ethic and the Victorian era, many people, especially women, decide that they don't deserve good sex. Even if they didn't always believe that sex was dirty, to justify any sexual problems they may have, they reach the conclusion that sex isn't right for them. That's nonsense. Everyone has a right to enjoy sex and not go around sexually frustrated. It's true that you may need to overcome some obstacles, but it's rare that you can't do this if you give sex the place in your life it deserves.

The Top 10 To-Dos to Keep Your Sex Life Active

1. Don't allow your hormones to set the rules when it comes to your sex life.

2. Try to discover the source of any relationship conflicts.

3. If you can't fix a relationship problem yourself, seek professional help.

4. Make sex a priority.

5. Learn how to push negative thoughts aside.

6. Engage in sexual activity even if the urge isn't there.

7. Don't let your sex life evaporate.

8. Maintain good communications with your partner.

9. If you need professional help, of any sort, make the time for it.

10. Don't adopt an attitude that sex isn't right for you, because sex is for everyone.

The Male Perspective

I've mentioned the changes that men undergo as they grow older, such as the loss of psychogenic erections, problems with erectile dysfunction (ED), and possibly even impotency. I know that this book is aimed at women, to teach them how to get the most out of their relationship with their gynecologist, but because I've talked so much about sex, and men are an integral part of your sex life, I want to say a few words about their side of the equation.

As many women know, men in general are hesitant to go to the doctor, especially when it comes to problems with their sexual organs. Now a gynecologist can't treat a man, but while every woman knows that there is a doctor just for her, most men don't know that if they are having any problems with their genitals, they should go see a urologist.

When a man comes to me with any sort of erectile difficulties, I send him to a urologist before anything else. I need to make sure that his problem isn't physical, because if it is, that's not something I as a sex therapist can treat. If I order a man to see a urologist,

99 times out of 100 he goes. Now here's where your gynecologist can help. If a woman has a serious problem with her ability to urinate, a gynecologist will send her to see a urologist. So your gynecologist has a relationship with urologists and can recommend one for your husband to see. If your partner needs to see a urologist, and you can supply him with the name and the phone number of one, the likelihood of his actually going increases enormously.

Let me add one last point here. The age at which a man may start to have problems with his erections varies according to his physical health. An erection is caused by blood flow, and it turns out that one of the earliest signs of a problem with a man's circulatory system, such as plaque buildup in his arteries, is erectile difficulty. So while ED can have an impact on your sex life, there's another very good reason for your partner to see a doctor about it—it could save his life. If you have to nudge him, I give you permission, because not only will your sex life benefit, but you may actually help him catch a serious health condition before it does him major harm.

AFTERWORD

Every day, scientists are making new discoveries in the field of health. It's difficult for even a doctor to keep up with all the news in his or her field, so how are you supposed to manage your health when it's practically impossible for you to fully grasp all the information that's out there? Luckily for you, you don't have to. The skills you need to develop when it comes to maintaining your health, or that of a loved one, are not the skills of a scientist but those of a CEO.

Does the CEO of a big company totally understand what's coming out of the R&D labs she oversees? Of course not. That's not her job. Her job is to make sure that all of the experts on that staff are working in a cohesive manner to further the benefit of the company. That's not necessarily an easy task, but it is a manageable one. What it takes are the following:

Know the basics. You have to have a minimal understanding of what the experts, in this case your doctors, are telling you and asking you. As I said in chapter 4, your medical history is something that you have to know inside and out, and if you don't, then make it your business to find out as much about it as you can.

Develop the ability to ask questions. When a CEO gets her staff into a meeting, she has to be able to pose the perceptive questions that will allow her to find out what's really going on and that will also make her people see her as someone who can digest the information they're giving her. In light of that, never go to a doctor's appointment without a list of questions. Your questions will let your doctor know that you take your health very seriously and will help lead to a better outcome.

Take initiative. A CEO doesn't sit back and wait for a crisis to develop. If she senses trouble, she calls her team together to straighten things out before they get out of hand. This concept is even more important when it comes to your health. If you feel symptoms, get them checked out. The longer you wait, the more damage may be occurring, and as we've seen in the case of some sexually transmitted diseases, damage can occur even if the symptoms go away entirely. It's your body, so you must be proactive about taking care of it.

Don't be embarrassed. A CEO can't hide behind her desk. The most important role of the head of any operation is to lead, and to do that, you have to put yourself out there front and center. When it comes to visiting a gynecologist, a lot of women allow their embarrassment about sex to keep them tongue-tied. But it's your body, and you're the one who is going to suffer if you don't speak up. Rather than be ashamed of your body and your sexuality when you're at the gynecologist's office, be willing to reveal all. In the end, you'll be glad you did.

Don't be afraid of change. One of the toughest tasks of a CEO is to initiate change. People get set in their ways and initiating change is difficult, and that's especially true when a CEO realizes that a key member of the team isn't carrying his or her weight. If you and your doctor, be it a gynecologist or any other type of doctor, don't seem to be working well together, then go for a second opinion. Maybe you'll decide that it isn't the right time for a change in doctors, but you also shouldn't look the other way if your health care needs some shaking up.

APPENDIX

Sexually Speaking Illustrations

These illustrations cover three main topics: the female reproductive system and genitalia, how to do a breast exam, and proper condom usage.

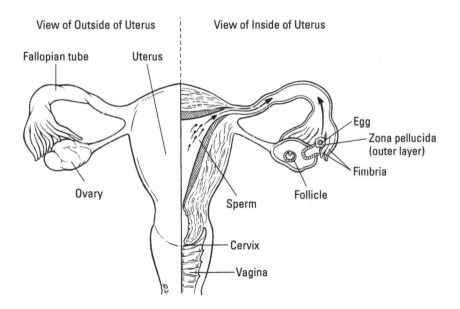

A woman's internal genitalia include the vagina, cervix, uterus, fallopian tubes, and ovaries. After sexual intercourse, sperm travel up through the uterus and into the fallopian tubes toward an egg that has been released by one of the ovaries.

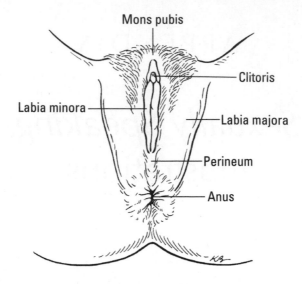

An exterior view of the vulva.

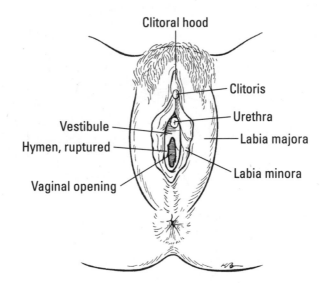

An interior view of the vulva.

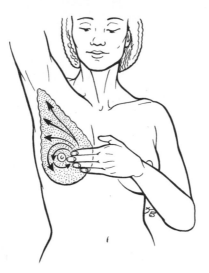

A monthly breast self-exam can detect signs of breast cancer in between your yearly visit to the gynecologist. With your arm raised overhead, gently palpate your breast with the opposite hand in a counterclockwise fashion. Be sure to also palpate the tissue near the armpit.

Leave space at tip

Roll it completely down the shaft

When used properly, condoms can offer a high degree of protection against pregnancy and STDs.

INDEX